FOLLOWING THE SAINTS

THE SAINTS: OUR INTERCESSORS WITH GOD—
The majesty of God is so great and above human beings that at times we approach Him through intercessors—His friends, the Angels and Saints. We ask their help in obtaining our requests from God.

Following the Saints

DIALOGUES, PRAYERS, AND DEVOTIONS
INTENDED TO HELP EVERYONE
KNOW, LOVE, AND FOLLOW
THE SAINTS

By

REV. WALTER VAN DE PUTTE, C.S.Sp.

Illustrated

Dedicated to ST. JOSEPH
Patron of the Universal Church

CATHOLIC BOOK PUBLISHING CO.
New Jersey

IMPRIMI POTEST: William R. Headley, C.S.Sp.,
Provincial

NIHIL OBSTAT: Daniel V. Flynn, J.C.D.
Censor Librorum

IMPRIMATUR: Joseph T. O'Keefe
Vicar General, Archdiocese of New York

(T-336)

PREFACE

GOD is almighty and could achieve whatever He desires without any help from His creatures. Nevertheless, He has chosen to make use of weak, fallible instruments such as we human beings are, not only for procreating the human race but also for teaching and helping us to serve Him properly and become His beloved children for all eternity.

At one time courses in history were principally records of wars, of the cruelty of human beings toward one another, and of their meanness in relation to God. Yet despite foreseeing all this, God chose to create rational creatures endowed with free will. For He knew that with His help a great number of human beings would become faithful, true adorers and lovers of their Divine Creator and charitable toward their neighbor.

Thus, a more complete history of the human race reveals God's government and guidance, His merciful love for members of His chosen people, and the unbelievable self-sacrificing love of the Son of God. Though He was God from all eternity, He chose to be conceived a man in Mary by the Holy Spirit, and to die on the Cross for the salvation of all.

Jesus Christ is the Holy One of God. Not only did He give us the example of a most holy life but He also gave us the supernatural power of grace enabling us to be adopted children of God, "other Christs" through being imitators of Christ, and members for all eternity of the Divine Trinity of Father, Son, and Holy Spirit. This is what it means to be a Saint.

Many Christian Saints are now living a blessed life with God, and it is certain that they are greatly interested in us who are still walking as pilgrims upon earth. Though mostly unseen and unheard, they can inspire us by what we know about their saintly lives and they are always ready to intercede for us with God. This is in accord with God's will, and we are foolish when we neglect such assistance.

What a variety of followers of Christ there are: those who died as youngsters or in old age, those who were Saints in their childhood like Saint Stanislaus Kostka, and others who became converts just before death, like Saint Dismas, the good thief who died with our Lord; Saint Peter who denied Christ and Saint Paul who persecuted Him in His members; Saint Augustine who fled from Christ for the world till he was overtaken and Saint Elizabeth of Portugal who found Christ in the world.

Inasmuch as Christ was unable to sin and Mary never sinned, we find it easier to relate to and imitate the Saints who both could and for the most part did sin (albeit lightly in most cases). Because they are so much closer to us sinners, and were successful in becoming holy followers of Christ, their example and their words and prayers can more easily encourage us as we endeavor to bear our cross and follow in the steps of our Divine Lord.

What those frail human beings fulfilled we too can achieve if like them we make use of assiduous prayer, devout assistance at Mass, reception of the Sacraments, and meditative reading of the Scriptures, and, last though not least, if we recall the inspiring things in their lives and implore them often to intercede for us.

Such is the purpose of this unpretentious book. By dialogues with the Saints we hope to enable Catholics to learn to follow them closely and in so doing to follow their Master and the Master of us all—Christ Who is the goal of our life.

CONTENTS
(Alphabetical Listing of Saints)

CONTENTS

MARY: MOTHER, QUEEN, AND MEDIATRIX—Of all the Saints, Mary the Mother of Our Lord is by far the favorite of all Christians, She has been invoked throughout the centuries by all classes of Christians for all types of requests, and her clients have invariably been heard. **10**

MARY, MOTHER OF GOD

1st century   Feast: Aug. 22

Follower:

DEAR Mother of Jesus, Mother of God, it is through you that we received the Savior of humankind. Christ did not make you one of the Twelve Apostles, neither did He ordain you a priest or crown you an earthly queen.

He made you the greatest, holiest, and most powerful mother, a universal mother for all the children of Adam. He made you Queen of heaven and the most powerful intercessor for us with God.

Saint Mary:

My child, we should always strive to do God's will in all things and to accept everything God destines for us and permits us to undergo. This is what gives the greatest glory to God and at the same time gives us the greatest reward.

Follower:

While on earth, you lived in obscurity in Nazareth, in Bethlehem, and in Egypt. But after your death and glorious Assumption into heaven, you have gained the acclaim and admiration of millions and have secured aid for human beings throughout the ages.

Saint Mary:

I am the handmaid of the Lord. I gladly accepted the hidden life in Nazareth and a participation in my dear Son's shame and suffering on Calvary as He brought to fulfillment the work His Father had given Him to do.

For God had been good to me. He had shown me that His ways are not our ways, nor are His thoughts ours. If we but unite our being to His, we will be filled with inner peace on earth and overwhelming joy in heaven.

Prayer of Mary Our Mother

M Y *soul proclaims the greatness of the Lord,*
 my spirit rejoices in God my Savior.
For He has looked with favor on the lowliness of
  His servant;
 henceforth all generations will call me
  blessed.
The Mighty One has done great things for me,
 and holy is His name.

His mercy is shown from age to age
   to those who fear Him.
He has shown the strength of His arm,
      He has routed those who are arrogant in
         mind and heart.
He has brought down monarchs from their
         thrones
   and lifted up the lowly.
He has filled the hungry with good things
   and sent the rich away empty.
He has come to the aid of Israel [the Church]
      His servant,
   ever mindful of His merciful love,
according to the promises He made to our
         ancestors,
   to Abraham and to his descendants forever.
                              (Lk 1:46-55)

Follower:

Blessed Virgin, my Mother and Queen, obtain for us the grace to follow you in life so that we may be with you in heaven.

Help us to hear the Word of God, as you did, and put it into practice after your example. Let us be united with your Son in life and in death so that we may be united with Him in heavenly glory.

✛   ✛   ✛

SAINT JOSEPH

Patron of the Universal Church

1st century   Feast: Mar. 19

Follower:

DEAR Saint, so many things are unique in Jesus the God-Man, in Mary His Mother, and also in you, in your life and role. From all eternity you were chosen by God to be the breadwinner of the Holy Family, the protector of Jesus and Mary.

Your marriage was unique and you were only the foster-father of Jesus. Not even one word spoken by you was preserved for us; we know very little about your life, and even less about your death in the presence of Jesus and Mary. We are told that you were a just man, which means you were righteous in everything. And you displayed unwavering obedience to God's will for you.

Saint Joseph:

I have to thank God forever because He granted me the unbelievable privilege of being the head of a family in which one was the Son of God and another was the Mother of God. You call me a "carpenter," but in my

14

time on earth many carpenters had a great diversity of jobs.

In the eyes of my countrymen, my marriage was a very ordinary one and very modest was my calling. But the way I see it now, it was sublime. I now have the privilege of seeing God face to face and share in heavenly bliss.

I also realize that I can intercede for people who are still on earth. However lowly may be the function of people on earth, they must keep in mind that God likes to have them as members of the heavenly family forever.

Prayer of a "Just Man"

IT IS good to give thanks to the Lord,
to sing praise to Your Name, O Most High,
to proclaim Your kindness in the morning
and Your faithfulness during the night.
The righteous will flourish like the palm tree;
they will grow like a cedar of Lebanon.
They are planted in the house of the Lord
and will flourish in the courts of our God.

(Ps 92:2-3, 13-14)

Follower:

Dear Saint, teach us to be faithful to our state of life. Obtain for us humility, self-effacement, and willingness to bear crosses.

Enable us to accomplish every work, no matter how humble, out of love for God and fellow human beings.

✛   ✛   ✛

SAINT JOHN THE BAPTIST

Precursor of Christ

1st century   Feast: June 24

Follower:

D EAR Saint, cousin of our Divine Lord, can any greater praise be given you than that of the Son of God become Man? "There is no man born of woman greater than John."

You yourself witnessed to Jesus when still in the womb, when Mary the true Christ-bearer visited Elizabeth. Humble and self-effacing, you prepared the way for Jesus Who is the Way, the Truth, and the Life.

Saint John:

Like Mary, what can I do but repeat: He Who is mighty has done great things for me. So my soul proclaims the greatness of the Lord. It was my privilege to see the Holy Spirit descend like a dove and come to rest upon Jesus.

I am also grateful to have died as a martyr, as a witness murdered by Herod Antipas whom I had reprimanded for his adulterous life.

Follower:

Dear Saint, you did not leave us any formal prayer composed by you, but how prayerful— as praise of the Son of God—are your words.

Saint John's Canticle of Praise

[**M**Y LORD *and my God*],
I am a voice in the wilderness;
make straight the way of the Lord.
I am not the Messiah.
The One Who is to come after me,
*the strap of Whose sandal I am not worthy to
        unfasten,*
He is the Messiah.
Behold, He is the Lamb of God.
This is God's chosen One.
He ranks ahead of me
because He existed before me.
I baptize only with water.   (cf. Jn 1:1-36)

Follower:

Dear Saint, how greatly we need to heed your call and follow your example today. Pray for us that by our conduct and our words we may lead others to the Way, the Truth, and eternal Life.

✢   ✢   ✢

SAINT PETER

First Vicar of Christ

1st century   Feast: June 29

Follower:

D EAR Saint, called Rock (Peter) by our Lord Himself to signify that you were to be the visible foundation of Christ's Church, we know more about you than about any of the other eleven Apostles.

Though you were a well-to-do fisherman, you agreed to leave your possessions behind and become a fisher of souls for Christ. This was at a time when there existed much lukewarmness among the Jews and great immorality among the Gentiles. Your success as a leader of the missionary Church is in itself an outstanding miracle.

Saint Peter:

I could never understand why Christ did not choose John the beloved disciple as His Vicar

SAINT PETER: VICAR OF CHRIST—Entrusted with the government of an emerging Church, Saint Peter made his headquarters at Rome, the center of the world of his day. Under his sure guidance, the Church flourished and spread far and wide.

19

on earth rather than someone like me. I was often angry, impetuous, vacillating (even in my faith), and I actually denied at one time that I knew the Divine Master.

How did I ever manage to guide the infant Church? I need not tell you how very much I received from Christ and the Holy Spirit, especially at the first Pentecost.

Follower:

Dear Saint, you did not leave us many writings, but we have plenty of your words that have been preserved for us. I would like to quote some of them now in the form of a prayer that is a profession of faith as well as an expression of your great love for Christ.

Prayer of Saint Peter

D EPART *from me, O Lord,*
for I am a sinful man.
Lord, You know that I love You,
You know well that I love You.
You have the words of eternal life.
We have come to believe
that You are God's Holy One.
You are the Messiah,
the Son of the living God.

Follower:

How greatly we need such a profession of faith in the Divine Savior—a profession expressed not in words only but also in our conduct, in our practice of the Faith, in our obedience to the present Vicar of Christ, your successor, the Pope.

Obtain for us the grace, dear Saint, to become true followers of Christ by imitating your life. Help us to do all we can by prayer, conduct and any other means to spread the Good News among all people, and in the process to be ready to give our life, as you did, if need be.

✣　✣　✣

SAINT JOHN

Beloved Apostle and Witness
to the Divine Word

1st century　　　　Feast: Dec. 27

Follower:

D EAR Saint, your name means "Yahweh is gracious." You were Christ's beloved disciple and you stressed the Divinity of the Word of God Who became Man.

You have recorded for us more words of the God-Man than any other evangelist. What a treasury of thoughts you have left us in your writings!

Saint John:

I am sometimes pictured as a sweet spineless person resting lazily on Christ's breast. Yet do not forget that my brother James and I were nicknamed "sons of thunder" by the Master, and assisted by our mother we urged Christ to give us high positions in His Kingdom. This was before we knew the substance of our Lord's spiritual teachings, and I regret making such a foolish request.

However, I do not regret stressing the *fact* that Christ, in Holy Communion, *truly* gives us His Body and Blood. How mistaken are those who claim that bread and wine are mere symbols at the Eucharist, and that the Mass is a mere dead memorial honoring Christ as we honor prominent presidents with statues and feasts.

Follower:

Dear Saint, your entire Gospel and other writings are virtually a prayer of adoration and love. Therefore, it is easy to put in the form of prayer some of your inspired words.

Prayer of Saint John

H EAVENLY *Father,*
we proclaim what was from the begin-
ning,
the Word of Life,
which we have heard, seen, and touched.
What we have seen and heard we proclaim,
that we may have fellowship
with the Father and with His Son,
Jesus Christ.
God is Love,
and he who abides in love
abides in God,
and God in him.

Follower:

Dear Saint, you were a true self-giving lover, not a selfish lover who in reality has no love at all. In our day, regrettably, there seem to be many of the latter type.

Teach us to express our love for God in constant obedience to His will and in a self-sacrificing way. Make us also prove our love for God by practical service of and selfless love for our neighbor. Such charity shows, as you recalled, that we are true disciples of Jesus Christ Who went about doing good.

✝   ✝   ✝

SAINT PAUL THE APOSTLE

Outstanding Theologian and
Indefatigable Apostle of the
Gentiles

1st century   Feast: June 29

Follower:

DEAR Saint, you are one of the most honored Saints in the Church and a brilliant exemplar of love for Christ and your fellowmen. After your conversion on the road to Damascus, you proclaimed Christ unceasingly by your words and also by your actions.

In all your writings this devotion to Christ is clearly visible and even more clearly expressed: "I resolved that . . . I would know nothing except Jesus Christ—and Him crucified" (1 Cor 2:2). Again: "It is no longer I who live, but it is Christ Who lives in me" (Gal 2:20); and again: "Be imitators of me, as I am of Christ" (1 Cor 11:1).

Saint Paul:

Even now as I look back on my life, I am still of the same opinion that I expressed in one of my letters to the Churches. I did not deserve to be called an Apostle because I persecuted the Church of God (1 Cor 15:9). True,

I did it out of ignorance. But it still was an act to be deplored.

Yet God in His great goodness bestowed His grace on me and gave me the light of His truth. All that I did and all that I wrote was the result of His grace and inspiration. To Him belongs the glory—not to me.

Follower:

When I think of all the magnificent things you have written for Christians of all ages, I find it impossible to even begin setting them down. A host of subjects go through my mind such as the Mystical Body of Christ, the bond of love, the mystery of the Church, and union with Christ.

Saint Paul:

Perhaps the best approach is to concentrate on the idea that God is so great and we are so little. This will keep us humble and enable us to see ourselves ever in the right perspective.

We could rightly dwell on the following text forever.

Prayer of Saint Paul

O^H, *the depth of the riches and wisdom and knowledge of God!*

How inscrutable are His judgments
and how unfathomable His ways!
For who has known the mind of the Lord,
and who has been His counselor?
Or who has given Him anything
in order to receive a gift in return?
For from Him
and through Him
and for Him
are all things.
To Him be glory forever.

(Rom 11:33-36)

Follower:

Dear Saint, thank you for your inspiring words. Help me to take them to heart and to act on them continuously in my life.

Obtain for all Christians the grace to follow you in being united with Christ and in proclaiming Him to others by word and deed. And enable us to arrive at His eternal dwelling place in company with you, where "eye has not seen, ear has not heard, nor has it so much as dawned on man" what great things God has waiting for us who love Him (1 Cor 2:9).

✣   ✣   ✣

SAINT MATTHEW

Apostle and Evangelist

1st century   Feast: Sept. 21

Follower:

DEAR Saint, you are known as Matthew but originally you were called Levi, which means "following." Christians throughout the centuries have come to know you well as Apostle and Evangelist by your wonderful Gospel, for the Church has constantly used it in her Liturgy.

At Christ's call, you immediately quit your job as tax-gatherer and started "following" the Divine Master. No doubt you had already learned much about Christ's miracles and inspiring preaching, and you went on to learn more.

How kind of you to write a detailed Gospel in the native tongue of your Palestinian countrymen, which later was translated into many languages.

Saint Matthew:

You are right about my desire to inform all my countrymen about Jesus, stressing the fact that He was truly the Messiah or Anointed One Who had been promised them by divinely inspired Prophets. I specifically pointed out, however, that Jesus did not come to establish an earthly kingdom, as some of them mistakenly thought.

So prevalent was this idea in the society of the time that even Apostles entertained it. This shows how worldly-minded our little band remained even after receiving clear and repeated instruction from the Divine Master. Only after His resurrection did our eyes see the Light.

Follower:

Millions have learned from you to appreciate the Beatitudes, to follow and love the Divine Master while bearing their own crosses. Also, at every Mass we recite the *Our Father* in the form and amplitude that you have transmitted to us in your Gospel.

Saint Matthew's Text of the Lord's Prayer

OUR *Father in heaven,*
hallowed be Your Name.
Your Kingdom come,
Your will be done
on earth as it is in heaven.

Give us this day our daily bread,
and forgive us our debts
as we forgive our debtors.
And do not lead us into temptation,
but deliver us from the evil one.

(Mt 6:9-13)

Follower:

How inspiring and consoling is this prayer left us by Jesus as an inheritance. God is *Our Father*. Hence, we belong to *God's Family*.

And we say "we" for we are all brothers and sisters, children of God. We speak of God being in heaven, although we know He is everywhere. For speaking of heaven elevates our minds to higher, divine things.

Nowadays, we hear much about liberty and equality. Help us, dear Saint, to bear in mind that our Lord's prayer deals with the highest and most perfect liberty, and our equality as children of God.

✦   ✦   ✦

SAINT MARK

Exemplary Evangelist
and Missionary

1st century   Feast: Apr. 25

Follower:

DEAR Saint, you were not one of the
Twelve Apostles, but how well you
learned—especially from Peter—to know, love,
and follow Jesus. You manifested your missionary spirit by bringing the Good News to
people in Asia and Rome.

You also wrote for the Gentiles the first
Gospel, pioneering a new art form by which
future generations could come to know and
love Jesus. In it you showed Christ to be truly
human, registering human emotions, such as
apprehension (1:44), anger (3:5), triumph
(4:40), sympathy (5:36), surprise (5:30), admiration (7:29), sadness (14:33f), and indignation
(14:48f).

But you also showed, from the beginning of
the Book, that Jesus was not merely a holy man
or a great Prophet. He was not merely a child
or son of God as we are. Rather He was *the
Divine Son of God.*

Saint Mark:

The Lord was very kind to me. He gave me a most saintly mother who made her house in Jerusalem a meeting place for Christians. What a privilege it was also to have Peter as my teacher and as my father, for he called me "son" in his First Epistle (1 Pet 5:13).

I was also fortunate to accompany for a time the great convert Paul, a marvelous missionary. Another source of inspiration was Barnabas, my cousin, with whom I went on various journeys of evangelization.

Follower:

One of the other features of your Gospel is the so-called Messianic secret, by which Christ refrained from openly calling Himself the Messiah to avoid having the people think that He was a temporal king.

Then at the climax of the Gospel, before the Sanhedrin and the high priest, Jesus openly declared His Messiahship. This sublime profession, combined with another text from your Gospel, makes a fitting prayer.

Prayer of Saint Mark

HOSANNA!
Blessed is He Who comes in the Name of the Lord!

Blessed is the coming Kingdom of our father
      David.
Hosanna in the highest heavens!
"I am [the Messiah, the Son of the Blessed
      One];
and you will see the Son of Man
seated at the right hand of the Power
and coming with the clouds of heaven."

(Mk 11:9-10; 14:62)

Follower:

Dear Saint, obtain for us the grace to ponder your Gospel and imitate your simple faith in Jesus as God and Man.

Teach us to accept our crosses as Jesus accepted His, so that we may grow into the kinds of persons that God wants us to be for this life and for the next.

✣   ✣   ✣

SAINT LUKE

Great Evangelist and Kind Physician
1st century   Feast: Oct. 18

Follower:

DEAR Saint, how can anyone fail to love you who so touchingly described in your

SAINT LUKE: INSPIRED WRITER—Under the inspiration of the Holy Spirit, Saint Luke composed two books of the New Testament: "The Gospel according to Saint Luke" and "The Acts of the Apostles." The second is sometimes called "The Gospel of the Holy Spirit."

Gospel Christ's infancy, the role of His most devoted Mother Mary, and Christ's compassion for the downtrodden, and who later on gave us in the *Acts of the Apostles* the history of the Infant Church.

You went from being a physician of bodies to a most compassionate physician of souls. Although you were different from Saint Paul, your missionary companion, you were also like him in your eagerness to convert all people to Christ.

Saint Luke:

That is true. Paul was a Jew, whose parents came from Tarsus. I was born a pagan at Antioch, and in that city I became a Christian —although not in the miraculous way Saul was converted on the road to Damascus.

Follower:

As a methodical historian, you tell us at the beginning of your Gospel that you carefully traced the whole sequence of events in the life of Jesus, from the beginning. And you wrote the Gospel to show how reliable was the instruction that had been given to a certain "Theophilus" and Christians in general.

Saint Luke:

I also considered it important to emphasize the great role of the Holy Spirit in the Incarnation and in the powerful impetus given to the leaders of the Church on the first Pentecost. He descended upon and brought grace to Mary and the Apostles as well as to a good number of converts.

The Church today needs a new Pentecost. Pray daily for this grace.

Follower:

Dear Saint, you gave us a kind of Gospel of the Holy Spirit in the *Acts of the Apostles*. It is fitting then to quote here a prayer inspired by the Holy Spirit, which you placed on the lips of the priest Zechariah and which has become a prayer used by the Church and Christians in the official Morning Prayer of the Liturgy of the Hours.

Prayer of Saint Luke

B*LESSED be the Lord, the God of Israel, for He has visited His people and redeemed them.*
He has raised up a horn of salvation for us
*   from the house of His servant David,*
just as He proclaimed through the mouth of
*   His holy Prophets from age to age:*

*salvation from our enemies and from the
hands of all who hate us.*

(Lk 1:68-71)

Follower:

Dear Saint, help us to be devoted to the
Father, the Son, and the Spirit, as you were.
Give us a love for the Word of God and a con-
stant desire to meditate on it.

Enable us to imitate the meek Christ, to
have compassion on our fellow human beings,
and thus be worthy of the name of Christian.

✛   ✛   ✛

SAINT THOMAS THE APOSTLE

Exemplar of Genuine Faith
1st century   Feast: Dec. 21

Follower:

DEAR Saint, you appear
in three episodes of
Saint John's Gospel. The first shows your
impetuous character but also your love for
Christ as you exclaim: "Let us also go [with
Christ to Bethany], so that we may die with
Him" (11:16).

The second shows your love of knowledge and your practical bent as you interrupt Christ's discourse at the Last Supper with the words: "Lord, we do not know where You are going. How can we know the way?" (14:5). You thereby elicit for us the beautiful declaration: "I am the Way, and the Truth, and the Life" (14:6).

And the third episode is the one about your doubt concerning our Lord's Resurrection, which concludes with you making the first explicit confession of His Divinity: "My Lord and my God" (20:25-28).

Saint Thomas:

The Divine Master was most kind in calling me to be one of His Twelve Apostles. By His grace I remained faithful despite my constant concern for certainty.

Our Lord had wonderfully instructed me and the others by word and example. We had witnessed His many miracles. And it was impossible for us to say that He ever committed the slightest sin.

Follower:

There is a strong tradition that you preached the Faith in India and were martyred there. You gave birth to the "Christians of St. Thomas."

You also inspired an apocryphal but beautiful Gospel known as the *Acts of Thomas*. It contains the following prayer that can rightly be called your own because it mirrors sentiments that you have shown in your life.

Prayer of Saint Thomas

O LORD *and Vivifier,*
   Your grace has achieved for us
all that You had spoken and promised.
Grant us access to the place of Your peace.
For You are our Vivifier,
You are our Consoler,
You are our life Remedy,
You are our Standard of victory.
*Blessed are we, O Lord, because we have
      known You!*
*Blessed are we, because we have believed in
      You!*
*Blessed are we, because we bear Your wounds
      and the sign of Your blood on our counte-
      nances!*
Blessed are we, because You are our great hope!
*Blessed are we, because You are our God for-
      ever!*

Follower:

Dear Saint, help us to imitate your love for Christ and your dedication to truth.

Pray for a renaissance of faith in the Risen Lord and make us strive to bear testimony (even unto death if necessary) to Christ, the Way, the Truth, and the Life, Son of Mary and Son of God.

✛   ✛   ✛

SAINT TIMOTHY

Zealous Evangelizer and
Faithful Friend

1st century   Feast: Jan. 26

Follower:

DEAR Saint, many are the things that make you most attractive. Your name (*Timothy*) means "respectful fear of God" and fits you perfectly. No wonder you became a most beloved and loving bosom friend of Paul.

The Apostle came several times to Lystra, your birthplace, and through his ministry you were reborn through Baptism—in company with your mother and grandmother.

Saint Timothy:

It was Paul who prompted me to become a true follower of the Savior Jesus Christ. My father was Greek and my mother was Jewish, but in order to avoid trouble Paul had me circumcised.

I know from personal experience that Paul was a zealous and indefatigable Apostle, always seeking souls for Christ. I was permitted to accompany him on many of his journeys, and I was also with him when he was a prisoner for the Faith.

Follower:

We are fortunate in knowing much about you through two letters that Paul addressed to you as well as through many other letters in which he mentioned you, whom he called his "son."

Paul was happy because you were well versed as a devout student of the Holy Scriptures. No wonder he desired to ordain you and made you the Bishop of Ephesus.

Saint Timothy:

Paul gave me wonderful instruction in what you call pastoral theology. His instruction of me as a shepherd of souls was that of a most loving and exemplary father.

The Lord gave me many great graces through this wonderful convert to Christianity who continues to influence millions. A learned man, he declared that he wanted to know nothing but "Christ and Him crucified."

Follower:

Let me quote from Paul's first Letter to you, which contains a prayer that can rightly be called yours, for it contains sentiments that must have been the basis of your spiritual life.

Prayer of Saint Timothy

G*OD is the blessed and only Ruler,*
  the King of kings and the Lord of lords.
He alone is immortal
and dwells in unapproachable light.
No one has seen Him
or is able to do so.
To Him be honor and everlasting power!
(1 Tim 6:15-16)

Follower:

Dear Saint, intercede for us that we may have bishops and priests who will follow in your footsteps and those of Saint Paul. Let us all be able to repeat those magnificent sentiments expressed by Saint Paul to you:

"I have fought the good fight; I have finished the race; I have kept the Faith. Now waiting for me is the crown of righteousness, which the Lord, the righteous Judge, will award to me on that Day—and not only to me, but to all those who have eagerly longed for His appearance" (2 Tim 4:7-8).

✢   ✢   ✢

SAINT CLEMENT OF ROME

Roman Missionary and Fourth Pope

c. 38-101   Feast: Nov. 23

Follower:

DEAR Saint, we do not know a great deal about you, but all that we do know is very good. You were the third successor of Peter as Bishop of Rome and the first of the Apostolic Fathers of the Church.

Your fame in the Church has rested on a host of books attributed to you in antiquity, but in reality only one of them—the magnificent *First Epistle to the Corinthians*—has proved to be authentic.

Saint Clement:

I was born in Rome, and you can learn from the Acts of the Apostles (16:1) that I was of Jewish extraction on my mother's side while my father was Greek.

Follower:

We know you owed your conversion—after God's grace, of course—to the instrumentality of Sts. Peter and Paul. These, like yourself, died at Rome.

Paul in his Letter to the Philippians (4:3) calls you his "fellow laborer." Hence, although you were not one of the Twelve Apostles especially chosen by our Lord, you were very close to them. Tertullian tells us that it was Peter who ordained you as Bishop.

Saint Clement:

After the martyrdom of Peter and Paul in 67, Linus became Bishop of Rome and Head of the Universal Church. He governed the Church for about ten years and was succeeded by Pope Anacletus in 76. After twelve years I, unworthy though I was, became Pope until my death in 97.

Follower:

Dear Saint, we have the good fortune to possess your inspiring First Epistle to the Corinthians, written to quell a rebellion on the part of some Christians against their local Church.

The letter takes for granted the authority of the Roman Church and her right to intervene in such cases, but it exudes peace and charity while encouraging discipline. It was highly esteemed by the primitive Christians and was placed next in rank to the Books of Holy Scripture. It contains the following beautiful prayer.

Prayer of Saint Clement

WE BEG You, Master,
be our help and strength.
Save those among us who are oppressed,
have pity on the lowly, and lift up the fallen.
Heal the sick, bring back the straying,
and feed the hungry.
Release those in prison, steady those who
falter,
and strengthen the fainthearted.
Let all nations come to know You, the one God,
with Your Son Jesus Christ,
and us Your people and the sheep of Your
pasture.

(First Epistle to the Corinthians)

Follower:

Dear Saint, inspire us with a measure of your missionary zeal. Millions today are taught the crass falsehood that there is no God and no life after death for human beings. They are daily bombarded with false maxims and false values.

Make more and more Christians desire to live as true followers of the Divine Master—the perfect example of life lived as willed by God—Whom you followed so well. Make more and more Christians willing to die as martyrs for the Faith if this is God's will for them.

✢　　✢　　✢

SAINT IGNATIUS OF ANTIOCH

Example of Martyrdom

c. 50-107　　　　　　　　　　　Feast: Oct. 17

Follower:

DEAR Saint, you were a convert to the Faith and a disciple of Saint John the Evangelist. Saint John Chrysostom says that Saint Peter appointed you as Bishop of Antioch and that you governed with wisdom, love, and kindness for forty years.

SAINT IGNATIUS: VICTIM OF DIVINE LOVE—
This great Saint is always remembered because of
his overpowering desire to offer his life for love of
Christ. His example has inspired Christians to live
better lives for Christ.

But you always longed to shed your blood for our Lord Whom you loved with an overwhelming love. When a persecution broke out in Antioch, you were condemned to be thrown to the wild beasts at Rome because of your unflinching dedication to Christ and the Church. In the year 107, during the reign of Trajan, you received your heart's desire and gave your life for our Lord.

Saint Ignatius:

You are indeed right in your analysis of my heart's desire. I longed to give my life for my Lord Who has done so much for us. But I was totally unworthy of the honor. It was only by virtue of God's grace that I found the courage to remain steadfast in the Faith and to compose the following prayer.

Prayer of Saint Ignatius

I AM *the wheat of God,*
and am ground by the teeth of wild beasts,
that I may be found the pure bread of God. . . .
I long after the Lord,
the Son of the true God and Father,
Jesus Christ.
Him I seek,
Who died for us and rose again. . . .
I am eager to die for the sake of Christ.

My love has been crucified,
and there is no fire in me that loves anything.
But there is living water springing up in me,
and it says to me inwardly:
Come to the Father.

Follower:

Dear Saint, thank you for your wonderful words, and for your magnificent example. Help us to obtain the grace to remain steadfast in the Faith in spite of the many trials and tribulations that may come to us.

May it please God to grant us also the grace to devote ourselves wholeheartedly to Him, and if need be even to give our lives for the Faith. In that case we know that you, Saint Ignatius, will be protecting us and receiving us in heaven.

✢   ✢   ✢

SAINT POLYCARP OF SMYRNA

Exemplary Bishop and Defender of the Faith
c. 69-155   Feast: Feb. 23

Follower:

DEAR Saint, there is something very attractive in you for many reasons. You became a convert in the first Christian century at an early age and you were instructed by Saint John the Evangelist. No wonder you had such a strong faith in the Divine Master and so ardent a love for Him.

We are told that Saint John ordained you a Bishop, and you became the spiritual Head of Asia from your Church at Smyrna.

Saint Polycarp:

I certainly will always be most grateful to Jesus for giving me such a holy teacher as John, His own "beloved disciple."

How forcefully this Apostle brought out that Jesus was not only the son of Mary but also the Divine and only Son of God. And he stressed constantly our obligation to love our neighbor and to try to sanctify other human beings.

Follower:

We know that you conferred with the Pope on the question of the date of Easter and combated the errors of Valentinian and Marcion, bringing many back to the true Faith.

Then you were ordered to deny Christ by the blind and unbelieving Roman authorities, and condemned to death when you refused.

Saint Polycarp:

How could I have denied my Lord and Savior? Naturally, my humanity made me fearful, but God's grace kept me strong. In the midst of my persecutors, I found a strength that I never knew I had. I was even able to compose the following prayer that comforted me in the face of death.

Prayer of Saint Polycarp

L ORD God almighty,
Father of Jesus Christ,
Your dear Son through Whom we have come to
  know You,
God of the angels and powers,
God of all creation,
God of those who live in Your presence,
the race of the just:
I bless You.
You have considered me to be worthy of this day
  and hour,
worthy to be numbered with the martyrs
and to drink the cup of Your Anointed One,
and thus to rise and live forever,
body and soul,
in the incorruptibility of the Holy Spirit.

Follower:

Dear Saint, we are told that the executioners found it difficult to burn you, and that your blood extinguished their fire when you were pierced with a sword.

Inspire more and more Christians to profess and also to spread the true Faith and the fire of Divine Love in a world that so greatly needs conversion.

✝   ✝   ✝

SAINT JUSTIN MARTYR

Great Philosopher and Saintly Theologian

100-165   Feast: June 1

Follower:

DEAR Saint, you were born about the year 100 and became a wonderful light, casting out much darkness in that century. At a time when the science of the defense of the Faith was so vitally needed, you became the first Christian Apologist.

You started out as a lover of natural wisdom, a philosopher using reason alone. For many years you sought true light, and you finally found it in Jesus Christ, the Light and the

Life of all human beings for time and for eternity.

Saint Justin:

Unfortunately, I did not have the privilege of meeting any one of the Apostles. However, since I lived in Palestine, I came in contact with the living tradition that came down from the Apostles and the saintly lives of many of their followers. I also had the inspired and inspiring Gospels and Letters. Finally, I received God's grace so that I embraced Jesus as my Savior.

Follower:

Upon your conversion you began your life of bearing public witness to Christ as an Apologist—one who defends the truth of the Faith before the people of the world.

How greatly we need today religious teachers like yourself who are well-versed in philosophy (both ancient and modern) and at the same time are well acquainted with the Word of God (the inspired Scriptures) through dedicated study and assiduous prayer.

Saint Justin:

That is true. People must learn to reason correctly, seek proper information about

Christ, His teaching, His commission to teach all nations, and His entrusting of such instruction to the Teaching Authority of the Church that He founded.

Not by bread alone does a person live but by every word that comes from the mouth of God. And this is transmitted to all people by the Church, the Bride of Christ.

Follower:

Dear Saint, you have also left us one of the earliest accounts of the celebration of the Eucharist as well as the text of an early Eucharistic Prayer. The following prayer tells us the main purposes of the Eucharist. May we also use it to sum up the main purposes of our life.

Prayer of Saint Justin Martyr

WE *pray together for ourselves,*
for him who has just been enlightened,
and for all others in whatever place they may
    be,
that we may obtain the knowledge of the truth,
the grace to practice virtue,
and the power to keep the commandments,
so that we may deserve eternal salvation.

Follower:

Dear Saint, you clearly proved your faith and love for the Divine Master by openly disseminating Christian revelation, although you knew full well that you thereby risked being put to death.

Obtain for us the grace to follow you in your witness. Grant us a love of Jesus and of the Faith that will impel us to give ourselves constantly so that Jesus may be known and loved all over the world.

✢　　✢　　✢

SAINT IRENAEUS OF LYONS

Example of One Who Teaches the Faith

c. 130-200　　　　　　　　　　　　　Feast: June 28

Follower:

DEAR Saint, you were born not far from the great city of Smyrna in Western Asia Minor. There you were instructed by Saint Polycarp, the Bishop, who had himself been taught by Saint John the Evangelist. Thus you were closely connected with the Apostles and the early Church.

You eagerly learned the apostolic teaching and went on to become a great defender of the Faith. Later on, you traveled to Gaul (France) where you worked under Bishop Photinus, who governed the diocese of Lyons. At his death you became the Bishop yourself.

Saint Irenaeus:

You are correct in what you say about me. I was very fortunate to know saintly men who imparted to me the very Faith of the Apostles with Jesus Christ as the cornerstone. In turn, I made it my task to communicate that same pristine Faith, unalloyed, to others.

With God's grace I composed numerous works, but only a few have been preserved for your age, for example, my books against heresies. I combated heresies because they distort the true Faith of God, and I endeavored to bring about a unity of belief on the part of all Christians, as you can see from the following prayer.

Prayer of Saint Irenaeus

FATHER,
give perfection to beginners,
understanding to the little ones,
and help to those who are running their course.

Give sorrow to the negligent,
fervor to the lukewarm,
and a good consummation to the perfect.

Follower:

Dear Saint, I admire you and your tremendous devotion to our Faith. Obtain God's help for us that we may get to know our Faith better and come to a truer knowledge of Jesus Christ.

In turn, let us be able to pass on the true Faith to others so that we will be doing our part to ensure that one day there will be one Lord and one Shepherd for all Christians united in the one Faith.

✢   ✢   ✢

SAINT HIPPOLYTUS

Priest and Martyr

c. 170-235   Feast: Aug. 13

Follower:

DEAR Saint, sometimes people are inclined to ask why we read the life of a Pope, or Martyr, when we do not belong to such categories. Yet no matter what our office or calling may be, we can learn from the Saints to be more faithful followers of Christ—for this is what they strove to be.

Though our knowledge of your life is sketchy, it is evident that as a priest in the early Roman Church you were zealous for orthodoxy and penitential discipline.

Saint Hippolytus:

Indeed I was. Unfortunately, my concern in this direction made me "more orthodox than the Pope," who is really the Voice of Christ. As a result, I came into conflict with successive Popes on these points: Zephyrinus (198-217) and especially Callistus (217-222).

Those who believed as I did went so far as to elect me Pope in opposition to Callistus whom I had accused of laxity and heresy. I know now, of course, that although I was in good faith, I was an antipope and the head of a schism against the Church during the reigns of the next two Popes, Urban (222-230) and Pontian (230-235).

Follower:

The important thing is that this was the only mark against you, and you atoned for it by resigning your "pontificate" and giving your life for the true Faith in union with Pope Pontian who also resigned. This happened under the Emperor Maximus in 235.

The Church rightly honors you for the good things you did as well as for your martyrdom. You composed the earliest known commentary on Scripture, that of the Book of Daniel, and you zealously defended the Faith.

You also wrote the *Apostolical Constitutions*, which contains the earliest known ritual of ordinations and is the equivalent of a Roman Ritual. It has proved to be invaluable to the Church and has gained enduring renown for you over the years.

Saint Hippolytus:

As far as I am concerned, the best thing I did was to return to the fold of the Vicar of Christ and to offer my martyrdom for my schismatic years—even though the schism was the result of a good conscience.

Prayer of Saint Hippolytus

CHRIST is risen,
    and death has been destroyed.
Christ is risen,
and the demons have been put to rout.

Christ is risen,
and the angels rejoice.
Christ is risen,
and no dead person remains in the tomb.
Christ, risen from the dead,
is the Head of those who sleep.
To Him be glory and power
forever and ever.

Follower:

Dear Saint, teach us how to live in troubled times. Show us that the only true beacon is Christ's Church and His Vicar.

Make us adhere to that Church and cling to its teachings. For it is in doing so that we will be united with the Risen Christ and rise with Him to eternal life in glory.

✢   ✢   ✢

SAINT ANTHONY OF EGYPT

Founder of Monasticism

251-356   Feast: Jan. 17

Follower:

DEAR Saint, model for religious whether they are hermits or live in common with

SAINT ANTHONY: HERMIT FOR GOD—Blessed with strength to give up all earthly goods for God, Saint Anthony of Egypt is the perfect exemplar of saving the world by renouncing its goods and pleasures.

others, you realized the great value of life in most intimate union with God, in assiduous prayer, work, mortification, and poverty.

Unfortunately, there are some people today who regard time spent in contemplation, meditation, and oral prayer as time lost. Even Religious have sometimes become lost in feverish work performed on the purely human level.

Saint Anthony:

Strange as it seems, there are even those who would criticize our Lord because He withdrew for forty days in the desert. They prefer not to recall that Jesus spent the whole night in prayer at times, and that He took His disciples apart to rest a while.

Mind you, this was done by the Holy One Who was both Man and the all-knowing, all-powerful, and all-holy Son of God. Saints Peter and Paul also knew how to take time out for prayer.

Follower:

Dear holy Abbot, we know that thousands have been edified by your saintly solitary life. Your Rule for monastic life must have been inspired by your living and loving association with the Divine Master.

In solitude with God—after the example of the man so highly praised by Christ, His precursor, John the Baptist—you grew in holiness and offered prayers such as the following one.

Prayer of Saint Anthony

L ORD,
   You know
who I am,
where I came from,
and why I am here.
I know that I am not worthy to see You.
Nevertheless, I will not go away
until I have beheld You.

Follower:

Dear Saint, through your intercession enable more and more human beings to be strengthened and comforted by means of meditative prayer.

Teach us the value of time spent in prayer. Slow us down so that we will be able to give more time to our formation in Christ—which is our primary task on earth.

✛   ✛   ✛

SAINT ATHANASIUS

Defender of the Faith and Exemplary Bishop
295-373   Feast: May 2

Follower:

DEAR Saint, our Divine Master told His
Apostles that they had to be His witnesses; and most of them witnessed to the Savior by
martyrdom. In the fourth century you too witnessed to the Catholic Faith.

You did it not through death but through
your saintly life and your many sufferings
incurred as a result of your constant battle
against those who taught the heresy of
Arianism. For that reason, you were exiled for
sixteen of the forty-six years during which you
were Bishop of Alexandria.

Saint Athanasius:

I lived in troublesome times, but I was not
the only Catholic who suffered. We did so
because we bore testimony to Christ Who is
the Way, the Truth, and the Life—not merely
a great Prophet but the only Son of God. Even
in your twentieth and twenty-first centuries
many have been persecuted because they wanted to live as followers of the Divine Master.

Jesus was killed after going about doing good. He was executed like a criminal even though He had performed countless miracles, brought the Good News to the poor and the downtrodden, and shown great mercy to the sinful. He promised all who accepted Him as the Divine Messiah and served Him that they would enjoy a blessed life with God for all eternity.

Follower:

You insisted on the Divinity of each of the three Persons in one God. So much so that for some ten centuries you were regarded as the author of the magnificent profession of Faith known as the "Athanasian Creed."

We know now that it was not written by you, but it was certainly a product of your inspiration with its emphasis on the divinity of all three Persons in God.

Prayer of Saint Athanasius

WE worship one God in Trinity,
*   neither confounding the Persons,*
nor dividing the Substance.
For there is one Person of the Father,
another of the Son,
and another of the Holy Spirit. . . .

The Father is God,
the Son is God,
and the Holy Spirit is God.
And yet they are not three Gods,
but one God.

Follower:

Dear Saint, today as you well know there are many Christians who have no devotion to the Holy Spirit. They should have such a devotion inasmuch as He not only was especially sent to human beings in a spectacular way at the first Pentecost but also remains as the "Animator" of the Church and individuals.

Obtain for us renewed devotion to the Spirit and unwavering Faith in the true Church of God, so that we may remain faithful followers of Jesus Christ till the end.

✣   ✣   ✣

SAINT EPHREM

Defender of the Faith

306-373   Feast: June 9

Follower:

DEAR Saint, I enjoy recalling your life for many reasons. You lived in a great century, when there appeared men like Cyril of Alexandria, Cyril of Jerusalem, Basil the Great, Augustine of Hippo, and the Emperor Constantine, who brought peace to the Church.

Much paganism was still prevalent in your day, and your pagan father—annoyed because of your interest in Christianity—cast you out of his house.

Saint Ephrem:

That turned out to be a blessing, for I was adopted by the Bishop of Nisibis, fully instructed in the Faith, and baptized at the age of eighteen. Our Lord was most kind to me.

I learned things about monastic life and was finally ordained as a Deacon. I chose to remain a Deacon all my life, recalling that Christ had come *to be a servant*, and He was supreme Lord!

Follower:

I know you liked to write both poetry and prose. Like the saintly Deacon Stephen who was martyred for the Faith, you became a teacher and defender of that Faith. Like Stephen also, you were inspired by the Holy Spirit and throughout the centuries you have become known as the "Harp of the Holy Spirit" as well as the Prophet of the Syrians.

Saint Ephrem:

We should never forget and ever trust in the power shown by the Holy Spirit at the first Pentecost. I know that it was only because of that power working in me that I was able to teach, preach, and write in defense of the Faith and to follow the Divine Master.

Prayer of Saint Ephrem

L ORD Jesus Christ, King of kings,
You have power over life and death.
You know even things
that are uncertain and obscure,
and our very thoughts and feelings
are not hidden from You.
Cleanse me from my secret faults,
for I have done wrong and You saw it. . . .
You know how weak I am, both in soul and in
*   body.*
Give me strength, O Lord, in my frailty
and sustain me in my sufferings. . . .
Grant me a prudent judgment, dear Lord,
and let me always be mindful of Your bless-
*   ings. . . .*

Let me retain until the end
Your grace that has protected me till now.

Follower:

Dear Saint, it is well known that besides your great love for our Lord you also had deep devotion to His Blessed Mother. She was, as it were, the Spouse of the Holy Spirit, through Whom she conceived our Savior.

Obtain for us a similar love for Jesus and the Holy Spirit and a deep attachment to Mary. Help us to propagate that love and devotion to others all the days of our lives.

✢   ✢   ✢

SAINT JULIUS I

Pope and Defender of the Faith

?-352   Feast: April 12

Follower:

DEAR Saint, those of us who have a special devotion to the Saints owe you a debt of gratitude. For it was during your pontificate that the practice of keeping a catalogue of the feast days of Saints came into vogue.

A Roman by birth, you were the Vicar of Christ from 337 to 352. During this particularly trying period, you defended the one true Faith and protected orthodox Bishops.

Christians were now free to practice their religion in the Roman Empire, but the Arian heretics went about attacking the true defenders of Church teaching.

Saint Julius I:

Yes, Arians had even begun to deceive the Emperor Constantine. When he died, his Empire was divided among his three sons: Constantine, Constantius, and Constans.

Among those who suffered at the hands of the Arians and were defended by me were Saint Marcellus of Ancyra and Saint Athanasius, powerful upholder of Christ's Divinity and Bishop of Alexandria.

Follower:

When you became Pope, the Arian Bishop of the East sent three deputies to accuse Athanasius of error. An investigation was held and he was declared innocent.

The Arians then asked you to assemble a Council at Rome (341). Once again Athanasius was found guiltless.

Saint Julius I:

The Arians, however, refused to accept that verdict. Therefore, I asked Emperor Constantius to convoke a Council at Sardica. This Council also confirmed what had been solemnly proclaimed at the great General Council of Nicaea.

I then wrote a letter to the Oriental Arian Bishops imploring them to accept the Apostolic Tradition that proclaims the right of the Holy See to be consulted. They had admitted this right in theory but slighted it in practice. They remained in the main unmoved.

Prayer of Saint Julius

M AY *almighty God
and His Son, our Lord and Savior Jesus
    Christ,
grant you His grace forever
in recompense for your marvelous faith. . . .
May there abide for you
and for those who come after you,
here and hereafter,
the better things
that eye has not seen,
ear has not heard,
nor the heart of man perceived*

but that God has prepared for those who love
     Him,
through our Lord Jesus Christ,
in Whom to God almighty
be glory forever and ever.

Follower:

Dear Saint, thank you for helping us recall the claims of the Pope in those early days of the Church. How safe we Catholics are since we do not base our belief on Scripture alone privately interpreted. Rather we rely on Holy Scripture, Tradition, and the guidance and interpretation of the Magisterium (Teaching Office) of the Church.

Grant that Christians may accept and live by the Creed that we proclaim every Sunday at Mass. Pray for a renewal of faith and truly Christian conduct in our day.

✣   ✣   ✣

SAINT HILARY

Bishop and Defender of the Faith

315-367   Feast: Jan. 13

Follower:

DEAR Saint, you were of a noble pagan family in Gaul, but you had an inquiring mind and a desire for truth. Thus, you passed smoothly from paganism to Christianity, from the study of philosophy to meditation on the inspired Scriptures.

You have left us a treasury of admirable writings regarding the Holy Trinity and other religious subjects. Even in our day, your works shed much light on Church teaching.

Saint Hilary:

I must say that the Holy Spirit gave me wonderful help to enter deeply into revealed truths. Through Baptism of water and the Holy Spirit (after I was already a grown and married man), a supernatural world was opened to my mind.

You might consider it strange that I was a married man when I was called to become a Bishop. Remember, however, that the Divine Lord called Peter, a married man, to become

Supreme Pontiff. And in my day the law of priestly celibacy had not yet become mandatory.

Follower:

You went on to become a great defender of the Faith, and in particular of Christ's Divinity, in opposition to the error of Arianism. But you were always kind to those who were in error, and could repeat the words of the Master: "Learn from Me because I am gentle."

This did not prevent you from using strong language—as was also done by our Lord—when that was found to be necessary. As Christ used harsh language against the hypocritical Pharisees, so did you use harsh language against the Emperor in his blind hostility to Christianity.

Saint Hilary:

Yes, our Lord used strong language even toward Saint Peter, but we must not forget that Christ is the Divine Lord. He knows perfectly what is in any person's mind and will.

We, on the other hand, are very fallible creatures who do not know what is in others. We judge by externals, and this always presents the danger of being wrong. We should strive to condemn attitudes, not people.

Prayer of Saint Hilary

O LORD,
  deliver us from the futile battles of words,
and assist us in professing the truth.
Keep us steadfast in faith,
a genuine and unadulterated faith.
Enable us to remain faithful
to what we promised when we were baptized
in the name of the Father,
the Son,
and the Holy Spirit.
Let us have You as our Father
and continue ever to live in Your Son
and in the fellowship of the Holy Spirit.

Follower:

Teach us, dear Saint, to accept and teach what is proclaimed by the Magisterium that Christ has established in His Church. Help us to follow our consciences, but make sure to form them rightly in accord with the guidelines of the Church.

Let us follow your example to go from natural truths to the truths revealed by the Son of God. And by meditating on them, let us grow day by day in the "Science of the Saints."

✝   ✝   ✝

SAINT MARTIN OF TOURS

Soldier of Christ

315-397   Feast: Nov. 11

Follower:

DEAR Saint, you are one of the most popular Saints in the Church's Calendar. In some places children pray to you and expect gifts from you in the same way that many others have come to expect gifts from Saint Nicholas.

You were born of pagan parents in Pannonia (Hungary) about 317. You served in the Roman Army and are famous for a legendary incident known to countless thousands. On one occasion while in Amiens (France) you encountered a beggar freezing from the cold in threadbare clothing. You immediately tore off part of your own cloak and clothed him in it. Later, Christ appeared to you and declared you had clothed Him with half of your cloak!

Saint Martin:

This vision of Christ climaxed a series of graces that worked powerfully in me, and I chose to be baptized after proper instruction. I found Christianity most wonderful.

Not long afterward, I received the call to lead a Religious life. I was ordained by Saint Hilary and even lived as a hermit for a while. I also had the satisfaction of witnessing the Baptism of my mother whom grace had likewise led to Christ.

Follower:

At the same time you had troubles. You strenuously combated the horrible heresy of Arianism and were flogged for it, but you eventually extirpated it from most of your area. However, you strongly opposed putting any heretics to death. When Saint Hilary returned from exile, you joined him once more and built a monastery at Ligugé.

There you lived until you were chosen Bishop of Tours. However, you continued to live a kind of monastic life even in that high position, practicing poverty and humility.

Prayer of Saint Martin

L ORD,
if Your people still have need of my services,

I will not avoid the toil.
Your will be done.
Indeed, I have fought the good fight long
        enough.
Yet if You bid me continue to hold the battle
        line
in defense of Your camp,
I will never beg to be excused
on account of failing strength.
I will diligently perform the tasks
that You entrust to me.
And as long as You command
I will continue to do battle under Your banner.

Follower:

Dear Saint, you were truly a soldier of Christ who fought for the Faith both by your words and by your actions. Many miracles have been attributed to you, but the greatest wonder or sign was your Christlike life that drew many to our Divine Lord.

Pray for us that we may follow you in our words and deeds, and so inspire others to live Christlike lives.

✢   ✢   ✢

SAINT BASIL

Intrepid Pastor and Doctor
of the Church

330-379   Feast: Jan. 2

Follower:

DEAR Saint, you were born at Caesarea in
Cappadocia into a family of Saints. You
are rightly called "the Great," not because of
worldly greatness but because you were an outstanding theologian, a learned Doctor of the
Church, and a wonderful orator.

Most of all, you were a faithful follower of
Christ and a most prayerful man. It is recorded that sometimes you spent the whole night
in prayer!

Saint Basil:

It is well to reflect that worldly honors are
fleeting and futile. Only true spiritual honors follow us beyond the grave. What a contrast there is
between the "achievement" of one whose corpse
is artificially preserved in a majestic tomb and
the solid achievement of millions of Saints, some
of whom have had their bodies completely
burned and possess no tomb of any kind.

Prompted by the Holy Spirit, I realized the vanity of worldliness and human-centeredness. Becoming a monk, I founded several monasteries and wrote a monastic Rule, which I hoped would help any Religious to lead a holy Christian life.

Follower:

How greatly we need your example and your teaching, dear Saint, We know you did not seek to become a priest nor were you ambitious to become a Bishop.

You were a man of vast learning but it was surpassed by your knowledge of Holy Scripture, which culminated in a burning love for the Divine Savior. You shine as a great light in the Eastern World.

Prayer of Saint Basil

L ORD, our God . . . ,
open our lips although we are sinners,
and teach us how to pray
and what to ask for in prayer.
You are the peaceful haven
for those who are buffeted by storms;
govern our lives
and show us the route to follow. . . .
Let us not be deceived by the charms of corrup-
tion

in this world.
Give us the strength to aspire to and attain
the enjoyment of future goods.
For You are blessed and praised
in all the Saints
forever and ever.

Follower:

Dear Saint, many today proudly praise the achievements of scientists whose inventions sometimes serve to destroy human beings and encourage the mistaken belief that there is no Divine Creator.

Intercede for all Christians, that we may inspire unbelievers to accept the teaching of Jesus Christ transmitted by the Magisterium of the Church and by holy Doctors like you.

✢   ✢   ✢

SAINT MONICA

Exemplary Mother and Widow

331-387   Feast: Aug. 27

Follower:

DEAR Saint, you were a most devout and devoted mother of the great Saint Augustine. All parents and all widows can learn much from you. Although your son was not a Christian for most of his early life and chased after the vanities of this world, you never gave up hope for his conversion.

Moreover, you uttered no recriminations but simply offered up constant prayer and acts of penance for his spiritual good. By dint of such efforts, you succeeded in obtaining from God the grace to see him become a Christian.

Saint Monica:

Do not praise me for my sanctity. I only did my duty as a mother. Realizing the immoral conduct of my son and his attachment to falsehood in religion, what else could I do but try to lead an exemplary Christian life! Did not our Lord say that this kind of evil can only be cast out through fasting coupled with prayer?

How can any true mother, and especially one who has received the grace of belonging to the true Church, not consider it necessary to storm heaven with constant prayers and mortifications!

Follower:

After your son's reception into the Church at the hands of Saint Ambrose of Milan, you resumed to Africa with him. Eventually, you died a peaceful death. And even till the end, you were concerned about the things of heaven rather than those of earth, as is evident by the words of the following little prayer that you expressed.

Prayer of Saint Monica

L ET my body be where it will;
God will raise it up on the last day.
One thing only I beg of you;
remember me when you celebrate Mass.

Follower:

Dear Saint, you are well aware of the disorders that have overtaken married life in our day. The abomination of abortion is demanded by mothers-to-be who thus contribute to the murder of the innocents. Then there are those mothers who neglect their Christian duties and are not solicitous about the proper Christian upbringing and eternal welfare of their offspring.

Pray that we may see a true spiritual renewal of family life. May it produce many sons and daughters of God who will glorify Him eternally.

✤   ✤   ✤

SAINT AMBROSE

Inspiring Teacher and Convert-Maker

340-397   Feast: Dec. 7

Follower:

DEAR Saint, how popular you became when you were Consular Prefect in Liguria. The people came to realize how gentle, charitable, and honest you were—and always ready to serve their best interests.

It was quite natural, therefore, that after the death of Bishop Aurelius Arianus of Milan crowds clamored for you as their Bishop. This was all the more remarkable since you were not even a Priest at the time. In fact, you were not even fully a Christian, since you were still a catechumen.

Saint Ambrose:

God works in strange and wondrous ways. He gave me great love for the truth and led me to serve His Church. He encouraged me to bring peace where there was dangerous discord, and to practice patience with uncouth and unpleasant persons.

SAINT AMBROSE: CHRISTIAN HUMANIST—A man of high culture and great compassion, Saint Ambrose gave the Church a strong leader and witness to Christ. He was a dedicated liturgist, an outstanding hymnologist, and a classical orator.

I learned to appreciate the wonderful example we have in Jesus, Who said that He had come *to serve*. We should constantly praise His generosity. He is the Lord of Peace, the Teacher of Truth, and the manifestation that God is Love.

Follower:

Accordingly, dear Saint, you were baptized, and ordained a Priest and then Bishop of Milan. In this post you shone as a great leader and defender of the Faith, converting many heretics. Later, you had the privilege of baptizing the great Augustine.

You liked simplicity and taught the people simple religious chants. Most of all, you sought God for yourself and to give Him to others—and you have left us this splendid prayer for seeking God.

Prayer of Saint Ambrose

LORD, *teach me to seek You,*
and reveal Yourself to me when I seek
   You.
For I cannot seek You
unless You first teach me,
nor find You
unless You first reveal Yourself to me.

Let me seek You in longing,
and long for You in seeking.
Let me find You in love,
and love You in finding.

Follower:

Dear Saint, one of the outstanding features of people of our day is that they are constantly seeking and questioning things. Unfortunately, many seek for the wrong things or in the wrong places.

Teach us to seek after God in the world and lead others to Him. Let us never be discouraged in this glorious quest, but rather realize that the act of genuine seeking is itself a guarantee that we will ultimately find God.

✝   ✝   ✝

SAINT JEROME

Scripture Scholar
and Eminent Translator

342-420   Feast: Sept. 30

Follower:

DEAR Saint, the mere mention of your name makes us think gratefully of your extraordinary knowledge of, scholarship in, and love for Holy Scripture. Your outstanding achievement was the translation of the Bible into Latin from the original tongues.

You are in a sense responsible for the great advance in Bible study among Catholics, and your very perceptive maxim is widely quoted and endorsed: "Ignorance of the Scriptures is ignorance of Christ."

Saint Jerome:

I was born in a small town near Dalmatia and gifted by God with a keen mind and a love for study. I learned Greek and Latin at Rome but became worldly-minded for a time.

Thanks to God's mercy, however, I overcame this lapse and finally accepted Baptism, becoming a member of Christ's Body and gaining a spiritual rebirth. I withdrew to a desert of Syria for four years, leading a life of sacred study and holy contemplation.

Follower:

At that time you also learned Hebrew and then went on to Antioch where you were ordained a Priest. Then at the invitation of Pope Damasus you produced the famous translation of the Bible known as the Vulgate and acknowledged by the Church as the only "authentic" translation.

You also wrote many Biblical commentaries in which you made use of a wide range of linguistic and topographical materials to attain the meaning of the sacred text. You were also a master of the art of letter writing.

Saint Jerome:

I must confess that I was a restless traveler as well as a restless student. That was my nature, and God was patient with me. I ultimately settled in Bethlehem, where most of my Biblical work was done.

Yet God gave me the grace to be aware that to put His word into practice is better than simply to read it. Hence, I tried to stay in union with the Lord through prayers like this:

Prayer of Saint Jerome

O LORD, *show Your mercy to me
and gladden my heart.*
*I am like the man on the way to Jericho
who was overtaken by robbers,
wounded, and left half-dead:*
O Good Samaritan, come to my aid.
I am like the sheep that went astray:
O Good Shepherd, seek me out

and bring me home in accord with Your will.
Let me dwell in Your house all the days of my
*   life*
and praise You for ever and ever
with those who are there.

Follower:

Dear Saint, how grateful we should be to you for, as it were, "opening the Holy Scriptures" for us and making them better understood and loved by us.

Inspire us to take God's Word seriously and put it into practice in our lives. Help Scripture scholars to interpret that Word with the aid of the Church, so that they will impart to all the true message of the Bible.

✛   ✛   ✛

SAINT JOHN CHRYSOSTOM

Great Orator and
Outstanding Bishop

349-407   Feast: Sept. 13

Follower:

DEAR Saint, you were a towering figure in antiquity and a living influence in your

own time. The title "Chrysostom" means *golden mouth*, and it was given you on account of the eloquence and glory of your preaching.

In a time when the spoken word was as effective as the printed word has become in our day, you gave your hearers "books" filled with instruction, information, advice, warning, and consolation.

Saint John:

I was born in Antioch and received excellent instruction in oratory. However, I learned greater wisdom while I lived a contemplative life outside the city.

Some serve God in retirement, in what is termed the contemplative life. Others are called to serve as shepherds of souls. But both have the same obligation to live in prayerful union with God.

Follower:

I recall that you were made a Bishop of the great city of Constantinople and spoke out fearlessly against the immorality of prominent people in your diocese. As a result, you underwent persecution, exile, and physical and mental sufferings. You bore them all with wonderful patience and for the love of the Crucified Savior.

Saint John:

As many have rightly said, we can win more souls for Christ by prayerful acceptance of sufferings than by eloquent preaching or by natural ability. For God brings much good out of sufferings of every kind.

Prayer of Saint John Chrysostom

O GOD,
   loose, remit, and forgive my sins against You,
whether in word, in deed, or in thought;
and whether they are willingly or unwillingly,
knowingly or unknowingly committed,
forgive them all.
For You are good
and You love all human beings.

Follower:

Dear Saint, Pope Pius X proclaimed you Patron of Preachers, not because of your powers as an orator but because of the humble and loving heart that underlay all your preaching.

Teach us to give ourselves to God with a similar humble and loving heart and to pro-

SAINT AUGUSTINE: GENIUS AND SAINT—One of the most towering figures in the history of the Church, Saint Augustine had many faces. He was a man of intellectual brilliance, countless friendships, pastoral acuity, and religious greatness.

claim His Good News to others through our words and actions.

✛   ✛   ✛

SAINT AUGUSTINE OF HIPPO

Wonderful Convert and Powerful
Communicator

354-430   Feast: Aug. 28

Follower:

DEAR Saint, you are one of the most famous people of all time and an outstanding thinker. In addition to your many great talents, God also endowed you with a most holy mother.

In spite of all that, you became involved as a young man in pernicious Manicheism, and your conduct became scandalous. But, prompted by your mother, you listened to the instructions of Saint Ambrose of Milan, and at the age of thirty-two you became a member of Christ's Mystical Body, the Church, by receiving Baptism.

Saint Augustine:

I returned to Africa and strove to live an edifying Christian life with the aid of God's grace. Bishop Valerius persuaded me to be ordained a Priest in 391, and in 395 he prevailed upon me to become his coadjutor Bishop.

Upon his death, I became Bishop of Hippo—but with the express stipulation that I be permitted to continue to live a monastic common life with my clergy. I did all I could to encourage the formation of Religious communities.

Follower:

How numerous, dear Saint, are your writings which manifest your love for God, your eagerness to learn, understand better, and then spread revealed truths. How powerful was your refutation of heresies, and how inspiring were your autobiography *(The Confessions)*, your sermons, and your religious treatises.

You have influenced millions for the better since your death at the age of seventy-six at the time when the Vandals were overrunning your diocese. Great has been your admiration for God's grace and undying your gratitude for the way the Good Shepherd led you into the one true fold. Your works are read more today than ever before because of your brilliance and your relevance.

Saint Augustine:

What can I say in answer to your nice words except: "The mercies of the Lord I will sing forever" (Ps 89:22) for it was His grace and His gifts that enabled me to grow both humanly and supernaturally.

I see clearly now how impurity makes the mind blind to the light that comes from the Lord of Lights. And when it is coupled with pride, with the obstinate determination to play with attractive falsehoods in religious matters, how difficult it is for God's Truth and Good News to reach an open mind and heart!

Prayer of Saint Augustine

LORD Jesus, let me know myself;
let me know You,
and desire nothing else but You.
Let me hate myself and love You,
and do all things for the sake of You.
Let me humble myself and exalt You,
and think of nothing else but You.
Let me die to myself and live in You,
and take whatever happens as coming from You.

Let me forsake myself and walk after You,
and ever desire to follow You.

Let me flee from myself and turn to You,
that so I may merit to be defended by You.
Let me fear for myself, let me fear You,
and be among those that are chosen by You.
Let me distrust myself and trust in You,
and ever obey for love of You.
Let me cleave to nothing but You,
and ever be poor because of You.
Look upon me that I may love You,
call me that I may see You,
and forever possess You, for all eternity.

Follower:

I want to thank you, dear Saint. Your exemplary life after your conversion is more powerful in its inspiration for us than sermons however eloquent and treatises however profound. Many today have left the Church and rejected her Divinely willed guidance.

Make readers of your works realize that by following your example they can learn to follow Jesus Christ ever more closely and faithfully—the One Who is the Way, the Truth, and the Life.

✛   ✛   ✛

SAINT BRIGID

Pioneer of Irish Feminine Monasticism

453-523   Feast: Feb. 1

Follower:

DEAR Saint, though you lived at a time when women had few rights, you overcame your status and became the pioneer of Irish feminine monasticism. You initiated community life for women.

So great is the esteem held for you that you are called "the Mary of the Gael" and are known as the second Patron of Ireland (after Saint Patrick).

Saint Brigid:

Indeed, my parents were baptized by the same Saint Patrick. Like other women, I was ticketed for marriage by my parents, but I felt called to the Religious Life. I wanted to become a Nun.

In God's good time, my desire was fulfilled and I received the veil from Saint Mel.

Follower:

But you did not stop there. You decided to bring together Nuns who before this lived alone. So you founded the very first convent in Ireland—at Kildare, "the Church of the Oak."

You were a prayerful, joyful person, most generous, and ever eager to help the poor. You once received a basket of excellent apples from a friend, and immediately gave them all away to the people around you.

Saint Brigid:

Yes, I did. And my poor friend said to me with a kind of sadness in his eyes: "But those apples were for you." I did not want to hurt my friend but could not help telling him: "Whatever is mine is also theirs."

Follower:

You were not afraid to take your place with the reapers in the cornfields. You also made butter, and you were renowned for your home-brewed ale—which accounts for part of the following prayer.

Prayer of Saint Brigid

I WISH I had a great lake of ale
for the King of kings,
and the family of heaven to drink it
through time eternal.

I wish I had
the meats of belief and genuine piety,
the flails of penance,
and the men of heaven in my house.
I would like keeves of peace to be at their dis-
    posal,
vessels of charity for distribution,
caves of mercy for their company,
and cheerfulness to be in their drinking.
I would want Jesus also to be in their midst,
together with the three Marys of illustrious
    renown,
and the people of heaven from all parts.
I would like to be a rent-payer to the Lord,
so that if I should suffer distress
He would confer on me a good blessing.

Follower:

Dear Saint, the Lord must have given you a great welcome at your death. Perhaps He even welcomed you in Gaelic. For it was He Who gave you your distinctively Gaelic character and virtues.

Pray that the Irish may continue to spread Christianity throughout the world. May they give the Church Priests and Religious who will be animated by the spirit of Saint Patrick— which was also your spirit!

✢   ✢   ✢

SAINT JOHN CLIMACUS

Exemplary Religious and Scholarly Hermit

579-649   Feast: Mar. 30

Follower:

DEAR Saint, we call you "Climacus" because you wrote a very famous book entitled *The Ladder (Climax) to Heaven*, which describes the thirty degrees to religious perfection.

You were a Palestinian, but unlike another Palestinian—the rich young man of the Gospel—you accepted Christ's call. Giving up your possessions, you followed Him more closely.

Saint John:

I chose to live a solitary life at the foot of Mount Sinai where so many Divine things took place, where Moses received the Ten Commandments. I remained there for forty years in loving union with God, meditating on the Scriptures and praying for my fellow human beings.

Eventually other hermits in the area begged me to become their head. I really did not want to assume the office of Abbot but I did so only because I came to the conclusion that it was what God willed.

Follower:

As a result, your holiness became widely known. Pope Gregory the Great wrote to ask for your prayers and he also sent useful things for the hospital that stood near Mount Sinai. It was altogether natural, then, that you should write a book containing hints for ascending the Mountain of Christian Perfection.

Saint John:

I tried to set down simple, short admonitions, adding examples that are greater stimulants than abstract reasonings. For instance, it is of the utmost importance to live in union with God.

This does not mean, however, that we must recite prayers all day long. We can obtain the same effect by renewing our intention, in our work and in all circumstances, to do all things and suffer all things out of love for God and the good of souls.

Prayer-Instruction of Saint John Climacus

PRAYER *is a holy violence that we use with God.*

The fruit of prayer
is mastery over the passions
and over the enemies of our salvation.
Do not become weary or give in to sloth,
but be strong in your combats.
Call constantly on the Heavenly King for help,
and you will have God Himself
as a Teacher in your prayer.

Follower:

Dear Saint, many moderns are human-centered and earth-centered without being God-centered first. Even when they believe in God, they live as if they didn't.

Inspire all of us to see God in all things and to fulfill His holy will every day. Help us to cultivate a solid prayer life, which will be of great help in our ascent on the Ladder to Heaven.

✧   ✧   ✧

SAINT JOHN DAMASCENE

Scholar, Hymnologist, and Preacher

c. 650-c. 750   Feast: Dec. 4

Follower:

DEAR Saint, you are known as the last of the Fathers of the Church. Born in Damascus (whence the name Damascene), you gave up a lucrative post at the court of the Mohammedan Ruler to become a priest-monk and live in obscurity.

However, because of the turbulence of your epoch, you found it necessary to go about preaching and defending the Faith. As a result, you are said to have written over 100 books. One of these is entitled *An Exposition of the Orthodox Faith* and has been favorably compared with the great *Summa* of Saint Thomas Aquinas.

Saint John:

One of the problems I encountered and strove to eliminate was the movement that wanted to do away with images of Christ, Mary, and other Saints. This was called Iconoclasm.

After reflecting on this point before God, I set down all the arguments against it in three Discourses. I pointed out that it is perfectly clear that we do not adore a picture that represents someone we want to remember, talk with, honor, and invoke in prayer. With God's help, this pernicious movement was stamped out.

Follower:

Your writings on the Iconoclast controversy even today form the substance of the Church's teaching on images. You were also a zealous collector of the thought of the Fathers who went before you.

However, you are probably best remembered for your contributions to Christian worship. You wrote many fine hymns including two Easter hymns that are still popular today: "Come, You Faithful, Raise the Strain" and "The Day of Resurrection, Earth Tell It Out Aloud."

Saint John:

I enjoyed writing hymns. It is an excellent way by which the faithful can participate in the Lord's worship and at the same time be instructed in the Faith. I am glad there is now more music in the Mass of the Roman Rite.

Follower:

You effectively defended the doctrine of the Real Presence in the Eucharist. And you proclaimed the Assumption of the Blessed Virgin long before it was defined as a dogma of the Faith.

This is what I especially like about you—your great devotion to Mary, the Mother of God, and to her pious parents, Saints Joachim and Ann.

Saint John:

It is sad that many Christians and even some Catholics have given up devotions to the Blessed Queen of Heaven. This is all the more lamentable inasmuch as Mary has shown her great love for human beings and her desire to help by her many apparitions and miraculous interventions in the last few centuries.

I wholeheartedly urge all Catholics to pray to her—as I did in prayers like the following.

Prayer of Saint John Damascene

H AIL *Mary, hope of Christians,*
hear the prayers of a sinner
who loves you tenderly,
who honors you in a special way,
and who places in you the hope of salvation.

I owe you my life.
You obtain for me the grace of your Divine Son.
You are the sure pledge of my eternal happiness.
Deliver me from the burden of my sins,
take away the darkness of my mind,
uproot the earthly affections of my heart,
defeat the temptations of my enemies,
and rule all the actions of my life,
so that with you as guide
I may arrive at the eternal bliss of heaven.

Follower:

Dear Saint, thank you for your inspiring prayer. Inspire us to say it often and entrust ourselves to our heavenly Mother all the days of our life.

Help us to spread this devotion to others and to make use of images to grow in knowledge and love of Christ, Mary, and the other Saints.

✥   ✥   ✥

SAINT JOHN GUALBERT

Exemplary Religious and Zealous Reformer

990-1073   Feast: July 12

Follower:

DEAR Saint, it has been said that the reformed Benedictine congregation that you founded was the most powerful single instrument in achieving the reforms of the eleventh century.

All of this was set in motion by your conversion in unusual circumstances. In one grace-laden instant, you changed from an uncaring nobleman to a dedicated servant of God and of your fellow human beings.

Saint John:

That is true. My only brother Hugo, whom I loved, had been murdered. In my anguish and fury, I vowed to kill his murderer and found the occasion for it on a Good Friday.

I cornered the murderer and drew my sword for the kill. But he fell on his knees and said: "By the Passion of Jesus Christ spare my life." This touched me so deeply that my revenge was swept away. I embraced him and went to a church to pray for him.

Follower:

What a grace that was for you and for the murderer! What you did shows clearly that you had learned to appreciate the sacrifice of Christ Who prayed for His executioners and all sinners: "Father, forgive them." And you then became a Benedictine, trying to atone for your worldly life.

But after a while you sought greater solitude. You visited a hermitage at Camaldoli and settled at Valle Ombrosa in Tuscany. There you were joined by others and built a small monastery in which you observed the primitive Rule of Saint Benedict.

Saint John:

Such was my remorse over my former way of life that I would not accept even Minor Orders. I strove to be kind to the poor and sent none away without some kind of alms.

I never forgot how kind God had been toward me in bringing about my conversion and letting me enjoy a true Religious Life. I thus founded many monasteries, insisting on the observance of what should be demanded of genuine Religious. I also worked for the spiritual welfare of the lay people who lived in the vicinity.

Prayer of Saint John Gualbert

MY *soul has thirsted*
for the strong living God.
When shall I appear before Him?

Follower:

Dear Saint, pray that we also may experience a true spiritual renewal of Religious Life in our day. May Religious refrain from living merely as social workers to the neglect of their own sanctification.

Teach them to follow our Lord's example and the fundamental rule He proposed to us: "For them I sanctify [and sacrifice] Myself" (Jn 17:19).

✛   ✛   ✛

SAINT WULSTAN

Faithful Religious and Exemplary Bishop

1008-1095   Feast: Jan. 19

Follower:

DEAR Saint, you are a shining example of the preponderance of the Bishop in the

Dark Ages. The Bishop was the all-around leader of the community, the sole lawgiver of the diocese, and the administrator of all property.

He was in charge of all social work taken on by the Church—hospitals, schools, and prisons. He was the principal judge and a kind of fiscal advisor to the great. Finally, he was the only one who could stand up to the king.

Saint Wulstan:

I know you use the term "Dark Ages" simply as an historical one, without any derogatory implications. But there are some in your day who like to downgrade my age by speaking sarcastically about the Dark Ages.

They fail to realize that there has been darkness in every age, including their own, when millions are taught that Christ is not the Light of the World and that in fact there is no God.

But, especially since Christ's coming, there have been great Saints in every age who reflected Christ's holiness and were truly led by the Holy Spirit Who is called the "Light of hearts."

Follower:

You were born in England and led the life of a Benedictine monk in a monastery at Worcester for forty-five years. The record shows that you were an exemplary Religious, remarkable for your humility, obedience, ascetical severity toward yourself, and kindness toward others.

As a result, you were chosen to be Bishop of the Worcester diocese, which you governed wisely and well until death. Religious life seems to be a good novitiate for being a good administrator and a spiritual leader who practices what he preaches.

Saint Wulstan:

Grace acted powerfully in me, and I always tried to follow the promptings of the Spirit. Accordingly, I was able to be God's instrument in putting an end to the horrible slave trade then existing between England and Ireland.

I always did my best to establish peace in a time of political troubles, and I was led to initiate the custom of pastoral visitations in England.

Prayer of Saint Wulstan

T O You Who have given,
    and Who are untouched by error or ignorance,

I render up my staff.
To You I resign the care of those
whom You have entrusted to my care.
To You I commit them with confidence,
for I know Your merits very well.

Follower:

Dear Saint, in our day we have a super-abundance of organizations and plannings of every type. But we seem to lack meditative prayer, regularity in spiritual exercises, and retreats that are not mere "socials." There is also a lack of obedience to the Magisterium of the Church.

Intercede for us that we may witness a truly spiritual renewal in the Church, one that can be said to be animated by the Holy Spirit Who so evidently inspired the early Christians.

✝   ✝   ✝

SAINT MARGARET OF SCOTLAND

Christian Queen and Model Widow

1050-1093   Feast: Nov. 16

Follower:

DEAR Saint, how well you came to deserve to be called "Margarita" which means

"Pearl" in Latin. Born in Hungary of the exiled English Prince, Edward, you quickly shone with Christian virtues. Christ was your Bridegroom and your Model.

Later, at the wise suggestion of your mother, you married Malcolm III, King of Scotland, thus becoming Queen of that country. You used your position, not to seek honors, but to serve the poor and the sick. You spread Christianity among the Celtic Scots.

Saint Margaret:

Everything you like in me I owed to special graces of the merciful God. For my part, I would have preferred a cloistered life, a life of prayer and mortification for the glory of God and the benefit of souls. My mother, however, saw that I could do more good as Queen.

Pearls are creatures of God and reflect light. What shone in me was merely the reflection of the Lord Jesus, the true Light of the world. Devotion to the Saints must lead to perfect devotedness to the Holy One of God.

Follower:

You knew the value of Religious life and founded the great Holy Trinity Abbey. Though wealthy, you lived an austere life. Your conduct showed that no matter what may be our earthly calling, our principal vocation as disciples of Christ is to bear witness to the Lord of the world.

You suffered much, and most patiently, from various ailments at the end of your life, and yours was a most holy and indeed most glorious death.

Saint Margaret:

The prayer I have left you provides clear demonstration that God brings good out of evil that is well accepted. At my death, all that I had worked for seemed lost. My beloved husband had been killed in battle and rebel forces were storming Edinburgh.

However, with God's help three of my sons succeeded to the throne in turn and reinforced the sacred work and brought it to fulfillment.

Prayer of Saint Margaret

P RAISE *and blessing be given You,*
   O almighty God,
for allowing me to endure such bitter anguish
at the hour of my departure.
For I trust that You are thereby purifying me
in some measure from my sins.

And You, O Lord Jesus Christ,
deliver me,
for through the will of Your Father
You have given life to the world
by Your Death.

Follower:

Dear Saint, the Prince of Darkness works constantly to inspire many to spread darkness in the spiritual order, and there are those who are continually seeking to extinguish the true Light of Christ.

Help us to look at you, precious Pearl, and invoke your intercession that we may obtain civil rulers who are honest and who trust not in themselves but in God. Raise up Religious and Laity who will be outstanding pearls broadcasting Christ's holiness.

✢   ✢   ✢

SAINT HUGH OF GRENOBLE

Exemplar of Obedience to God's Will

1052-1132   Feast: Apr. 1

Follower:

DEAR Saint, we often recall the words of the Angel to Mary at the Annunciation:

"Full of grace," which some express by "greatly favored one." Of course, Mary is the most favored of all merely human creatures.

But you too from early childhood appeared much favored by God. And it would have been most natural for you to consecrate yourself to God wholly in the strictest of Religious Orders.

Saint Hugh:

One great Religious Founder has said: "Be before the Holy Spirit (the Divine Inspirer) like a light feather before the slightest breath of wind." This is the attitude I adopted and tried to maintain throughout my life.

Let us remember that Mary expressed a similar attitude by adding: "Be it done to me according to your word." She, of course, became the Spouse of the Holy Spirit and the Mother of God.

Follower:

You were ordained and came under the wing of Bishop Hugh, who entrusted you with most important affairs. Though drawn to the Religious Life, you were told at the local Council of Avignon to accept becoming the Bishop of Grenoble, a city in sad straits.

You accepted out of obedience and were faced with an herculean task. However, as a prayerful man you knew that you could do everything God wanted you to do—through His help. And the fact is that you literally transformed the diocese in a short time.

Saint Hugh:

After two years, I resigned my Bishopric to enter the novitiate of the Benedictines of Cluny, but the Pope did not concur and told me to return to my diocese. Of course, I returned. Rome had spoken; the case was closed.

Follower:

Like a "feather," you offered no resistance. We recall that it was to you that Saint Bruno and his six companions came in their desire to forsake the world. You directed them to the desert of Chartreuse, and it was there that they founded the famous Carthusian Order.

In spite of your own love for that kind of life, you obediently followed the desire of the Holy Father, which you knew expressed God's will for you.

Prayer of Saint Hugh

VANITY *and inordinate affections alone are enough to cause the loss of salvation.*

SAINT FRANCIS OF ASSISI: DIVINE LOVER—
Overwhelmed by God's love for us, Saint Francis
gave up everything and became a troubadour of
that Love to all people. His example of love for all
creatures has inspired millions over the ages.

Only through God's mercy
can we hope to be saved,
and we should never cease to implore it!

Follower:

Dear Saint, how greatly we need to obey legitimate religious authority, as you have done!

Instead of constantly desiring to change things, may we strive to reform ourselves spiritually and work prayerfully for a true reform of family life and the life of religious.

✟   ✟   ✟

SAINT FRANCIS OF ASSISI

Ardent Lover of God and All His Creatures

1182-1226   Feast: Oct. 4

Follower:

DEAR Saint, you are probably the most popular and universally loved Saint. You were first named John but later called Francis (because of your father's French origin) to which was added "of Assisi," your birthplace.

This was also the place of your death in 1226, which means you were then only 44 years old! You have remained very well known to non-Catholics and Catholics alike. Some, however, merely connect you with birds, to whom it is said you preached one day.

Saint Francis:

I could also have been called "Rich" or "Richard" because my father was a wealthy man. But Rich I did not desire to remain and I have come to be called "The Poor One." Through God's grace and the inspiration of the Holy Spirit ("Father of the poor") I came to see the foolishness of attachment to and quasi-worship of riches.

"You can't take it with you" is a popular and very true saying. A Nun who had taught many wealthy children said one day: "There is no greater misfortune than to have a fortune." Yet with God's help wealthy people can be still detached from their wealth and use it to create jobs and give alms.

Follower:

In a short time, you accomplished unbelievably much—and you did so without depending on money. You realized, like Saint Paul, that you could do everything God wanted you to do in and through Him Who strengthened you. What was fundamental in attracting followers and converting sinners was *your wonderful example as another Christ.*

Saint Francis:

In 1210 I had twelve companions, which could make you think of Christ's Twelve Apostles. Pope Innocent III gladly approved my "congregation," which aimed at taking as its Constitution and Rule *the Holy Gospel.* Humility together with poverty and charity lay at its foundation. So we chose to be called *Friars Minor,* that is, little brothers.

Follower:

I note that you never accepted to be ordained a Priest. This too revealed your great humility. Neither did you and your Religious brothers remain cloistered. You went out to the ways and byways and like John the Baptist called people to repent for their sins, after fully accepting to believe in Jesus Christ and follow in His steps.

Saint Francis:

Avarice is the source of many sins. It is a kind of idolatry. Out of love for money, Judas fell away. The others, poor fisherman, remained faithful and won many souls for Christ.

Prayer of Saint Francis of Assisi

L ORD,
    make me an instrument of Your peace.
Where there is hatred, let me sow love.
Where there is injury, let me sow pardon.
Where there is friction, let me sow union.
Where there is error, let me sow truth.
Where there is doubt, let me sow faith.
Where there is despair, let me sow hope.
Where there is darkness, let me sow light.
Where there is sadness, let me sow joy.

O Divine Master,
grant that I may not so much seek
to be consoled as to console,
to be understood as to understand,
to be loved as to love.
For it is in giving that we receive.
It is in pardoning that we are pardoned.
It is in dying that we are born to eternal life.

Follower:

Dear Saint, we are also aware of your ardent love for Jesus Crucified, which found expression even in your wounded body. Inspire Priests, Religious, and Laity with that same love after your example.

Make those who accept you as their Father truly represent you in this age, which is growing increasingly poor in practical love for the Son of God, Who voluntarily chose to become a poor servant for the glory of God and the sanctification of souls.

✣   ✣   ✣

SAINT HYACINTH OF POLAND

Zealous Missionary and Apostle of the North
1185-1257   Feast: Aug. 17

Follower:

DEAR Saint, you must have rejoiced greatly when in 1978 a Bishop of Cracow in Poland became the Supreme Pontiff of the Catholic Church, the Vicar of Christ on earth. For you were born in Silesia, which in your day was a part of Poland.

After studying at Cracow, Prague, and Bologna, you earned the degrees of doctor of laws and doctor of theology and became a Canon at the Cathedral of Cracow.

Saint Hyacinth:

The Bishop of Cracow in my time was most kind to me. He made me assistant in the administration of that diocese. My uncle Yvo became the next Bishop and took me and another nephew, Ceslas, to Rome.

Who could have thought at that time (1218) that 760 years later Bishop Wojtyla of Cracow would also go to Rome to assist at a Conclave and would then be chosen as Head of the Universal Church.

Follower:

You had the good fortune of meeting the wonderful Saint Dominic in Rome, and inspired by him you became a Dominican and received the religious habit from that holy Founder. The religious authorities must have been impressed by your holiness, for you were permitted to make your vows after only six months spent in the novitiate.

Saint Hyacinth:

Attribute any spiritual goodness found in me to God's merciful kindness toward me. Together with a few others and as their superior, I was then sent to our mission. On our way to Poland we preached the Gospel in many places and received many who became members of the Dominican Order.

After a very lengthy journey we arrived in Poland and were received with great manifestations of joy by the people there.

Follower:

Here again, we cannot refrain from pointing out history repeating itself. For we remember the spectacular reception given in 1979 to Bishop Karol Wojtyla of Cracow after he had been proclaimed Pope John Paul II.

As we recall your missionary life we are reminded of Saint Paul's missionary journeys. You went about preaching the Gospel in the Northern Countries, Prussia, Pomerania, Denmark, Sweden, and Norway. You labored in Russia, and you even went to China and Tibet.

Prayer of Saint Hyacinth

D*EAR Lord,*
my brother is no longer an imperfect man.
His soul has reached the measure of perfection that you assigned for him
from all eternity.

Follower:

Dear Saint, how strange that so many today labor very hard to spread a false religion and even godlessness, while we who have the truth stand idly by.

Inspire many to become like you in sanctifying and sacrificing themselves to spread the true Faith. Intercede for us that the Holy Spirit may animate us as He animated you.

✢   ✢   ✢

SAINT CLARE

Model Religious
and Foundress

1193-1253   Feast: Aug. 11

Follower:

DEAR Saint, you are known as the patroness of television workers and are also invoked against "sore eyes." Indeed, by your exemplary behavior you have made many see clearly the great beauty of life wholly consecrated to Christ, in poverty, chastity, and obedience.

You are, as it were, a living broadcast of the sanctity of Christ to the ages. You are also the splendid counterpart of Saint Francis of Assisi, a man who bore the Stigmata, making people realize how much Christ chose to suffer for sinful humanity.

Saint Clare:

It was truly a privilege for me to have been born and to live in Assisi, a town whose name is forever linked to that wonderful man. Not only did Francis so radically leave the world but he also drew countless persons to follow him and thus become followers of Jesus Christ, the Poor Man of Nazareth.

God used Francis to make me try to do the same. He first placed me in a Benedictine monastery and, quite naturally, some of my relatives and friends tried to dissuade me from doing "such a foolish thing."

Follower:

However, you knew the means to persevere. Prayer and mortification strengthened your resolution and you saw ever more clearly the value of the contemplative life. It is not a selfish withdrawal from the world but a life in which one willingly suffers and prays for the supernatural welfare of all people.

You learned to see the beauty of vicarious satisfaction, completing in yourself what is wanting in the Sufferings of Christ, as Saint Paul dares to say (Col 1:24).

Saint Clare:

Our Lord used Francis as an instrument to make me cooperate with Him in the foundation of the Second Order of Saint Francis. In this way, my name became attached to an Order of Religious Nuns, as his name was attached to the Order of Franciscans.

Follower:

You were also blessed by God with a wonderful faith. Among other things, you believed that Christ not only is truly present at the time of the Consecration and Holy Communion of the Sacrifice of the Mass but remains present in our tabernacles.

Our churches are thus truly houses of God. This faith is clearly revealed by the fact that on one occasion you brought the monstrance that contained the Sacred Host to a window, showing it to men who intended to break into your convent and perhaps destroy it. They fled in terror.

Saint Clare:

It is perfectly clear that the first Christians believed what you said. Some brought Holy Communion to the sick, while others were even permitted to keep the Blessed Sacrament in their homes for similar purposes.

Prayer of Saint Clare

*D*EAR *Lord God,*
protect this city,
for it gives us our living
out of love for You.

Follower:

Dear Saint, pray that in the flush of the New Mass people will not forget the reverence that is needed in the presence of the Almighty. And inspire Catholics to visit, adore, and find consolation in the Divine Savior Who remains in our churches.

Help Orders and Congregations to be once more Religious houses where Religious are truly happy because they are faithful to their vows of poverty, chastity, and obedience.

✛ ✛ ✛

SAINT ZITA

Patron of Domestics

1218-1278   Feast: Apr. 27

Follower:

*D*EAR Saint, worldlings often fail to admire faithful domestics or servants. They bow before those who occupy high positions, even when these lead immoral lives. You, your sister, and your uncle were brought up in a truly Christian family.

Your uncle became a Cistercian and your sister chose the life of a hermit. You saw clearly that one can do God's will when exercising the most humble functions in the world by always following the guidance of the Holy Spirit. After all, our Lady proclaimed herself a "handmaid" of the Lord, and this she did as a mother in a household.

Saint Zita:

When God placed us on earth, He wanted us to do work of some kind. Joseph was a carpenter, Mary was a homemaker, and Jesus also engaged in carpentry. My parents worked properly, and their life taught me even better than their words.

Too many couples fail to give a good Christian education in the home. Parents must inspire their offspring to live as children of God. It was because of my exemplary parents that I chose to become a domestic for a well-to-do family.

Follower:

You were a model domestic and in reality became the Patroness of domestics. For forty-eight years you worked with perfect devotedness in that family.

You always found time for spiritual exercises, attended Mass daily, and led a life of loving union with God. You knew that Christ had said that He had come not to be served but to serve.

Saint Zita:

I can say in all truth that I tried never to lose time. I never refused to do extra work. This, of course, did not please the other domestics, but I tried to practice patience in their regard.

We who are now in eternity are aware that some "workers" do a minimum of work and then ask for a maximum wage. Others pass the time in idleness whenever they are unobserved and naturally find time for gossip.

Words of Saint Zita

A DOMESTIC *is not good if she lacks industriousness. Work-shy piety*

SAINT BONAVENTURE: SPIRITUAL MASTER—
As his name indicates, Saint Bonaventure has
been a bearer of spiritual "good fortune" for multitudes. His works form a golden treasury of Divine
enlightenment for all Catholics.

*in people of our position
is sham piety.*

Follower :

Dear Saint, you know that in our age people have lost the sense of "honest pride in one's work." They have the attitude that anything goes so long as they get paid at the end of the week.

Inspire more and more Christians to follow your example. Let them learn by experience that God can also be found in their work. Help them to realize that by their work—no matter how menial—they are building the world and getting it ready for Christ's Coming. And in so doing they will learn how true are Christ's words that *"there is greater happiness in giving than in receiving"* (Acts 20:35).

✝   ✝   ✝

SAINT BONAVENTURE

Seraphic Doctor: Master of the Spiritual Life

1218-1274   Feast: July 15

Follower:

D EAR Saint, like Thomas Aquinas you were one of the outstanding lights of the Thirteenth Century (termed the "Greatest of Christian Centuries"). You were called the "Seraphic Doctor" because of your ardent love for God. In your writings you made profuse and proficient use of the Scriptures and are rightly regarded as a Master of the Spiritual Life (the Science of the Saints).

Christened as "John," you received the name "Bonaventure" as a result of a remark of Saint Francis of Assisi when he was asked by your mother to pray for you who were very ill. Concerning your future, he exclaimed: "*O buona ventura*—O good fortune." This proved to be prophetic regarding what you were going to accomplish.

Saint Bonaventure:

My cure must have been a great consolation to my mother who was a good Christian, for I had the privilege of being reared in a truly Catholic family.

Moved by God's grace, I joined the Franciscan Order when I was twenty-two years old. After making my Religious vows, I was sent to Paris to complete my studies under the renowned English Franciscan Alexander of Hales.

Follower:

After the death of that teacher you studied under John of La Rochelle. In Paris you became acquainted with Saint Thomas Aquinas, and both of you struck up a close friendship and also befriended Saint Louis of France. What a wonderful and saintly trio you thus formed.

Saint Bonaventure:

Against my inclinations, at the age of thirty-five I was chosen Master General of the Franciscan Order (Friars Minor). I took office surrounded by dissension in the ranks.

Follower:

Yet, because of your gentleness and evident charity, you were successful in restoring calm. You had great devotion to Saint Anthony of Padua whose relics you returned to the place where they more truly deserved to be.

Saint Bonaventure:

Pope Clement named me Bishop of York, but I begged him not to force me to accept that dignity. Pope Gregory X later obliged me to become a Cardinal and Bishop of Albano.

One of my major sorrows in life was the death of Thomas Aquinas as he was traveling to take part in the Second Council of Lyons.

Follower:

You reached Lyons and directed affairs at the Council. You worked hard to make Oriental members of the clergy reunite with the Holy See. You were temporarily successful but you died from exhaustion, following Thomas into eternity by four short months.

Prayer of Saint Bonaventure

L *ORD Jesus Christ, . . .*
may my soul always revolve around You,
seek You,
and find You.
Help it to turn to You,
and reach You.
Let its every thought and word be centered
on You.

Grant that my soul may sing Your praise
and the glory of Your holy Name
with humility and reserve,
with love and joy,
with ease and gentleness,
with patience and tranquility,

*with success and persistence
to the very end.*

Follower:

Dear Saint, what a reunion you must have had with Saint Thomas when you were received by our Lord, whom you both had served with such deep devotion and fidelity. What a contrast between such holy deaths and the deaths of some political rulers who have served not God but their own insane ambitions.

Pray that we may have spiritually-minded leaders and that the Science of the Saints will become known to and practiced by countless Christians.

✣   ✣   ✣

SAINT THOMAS AQUINAS

Supreme Theologian and Angelic Doctor

1225-1274   Feast: Jan. 28

Follower:

DEAR Saint, in you there is no sign of the tension between the religious and the intellectual life that afflicts some people in our day. Your sanctity was achieved in and

SAINT THOMAS AQUINAS: THE ANGELIC DOC-TOR—A man of action but also of prayer, Saint Thomas set forth a masterful theological system. He also left us very beautiful prayers and hymns in honor of the Blessed Sacrament.

through the main work of your life—your intellectual activity.

For you knew how to remain humble despite your great intellectual exploits and sought only union with our Lord. As a result, you were thought to be stupid in school and even called the "Dumb Ox." But such dumbness is the wisdom of Saints, and your freedom from sin earned for you the name of "Angelic Doctor."

Saint Thomas:

That is true. I came to regard all that I had written as so much straw compared with what God had shown and revealed to me in a vision. Not that I deserved such graces—but it pleased Him to make use of me for His greater glory and the salvation of souls.

At another time our Lord was kind enough to appear to me and say: "You have written well about Me, Thomas. What reward do you desire to receive?" What a stupendous thing— that the Lord of all should accede to the desires of a lowly creature! I could only exclaim with joy: "I desire nothing but You, my Lord!"

Follower:

From early youth you were full of love for God Whom you desired to know ever better. You were also most eager to spread the proper interpretation of revealed Truth. You constantly refuted false doctrines and answered countless objections in matters of faith.

Your devotion to the precious Reality of the Holy Eucharist was outstanding. And even though you had studied at the famous centers of learning in Paris, Bologna, and Rome, you declared that you learned more from the Crucifix than from books.

Saint Thomas:

It is true that I accepted the truths expressed by philosophers like Aristotle, and indeed that I "Christianized" their works. Yet it is even truer that whatever I taught in lectures and in writings I learned principally through prayerful meditation on the Crucifix and on God's revealed Word or in the presence of the Blessed Sacrament.

Prayer of Saint Thomas
Before the Blessed Sacrament

H*IDDEN God, devoutly I adore You,
Truly present underneath these veils:*

All my heart subdues itself before You,
Since it all before You faints and fails.

Not to sight, or taste, or touch be credit,
Hearing only do we trust secure;
I believe, for God the Son has said it—
Word of Truth that ever shall endure.

On the cross was veiled Your Godhead's
*   splendor,*
Here Your manhood lies hidden too;
Unto both alike my faith I render,
And, as sued the contrite thief, I sue.

Though I look not on Your wounds with
*   Thomas,*
You, my Lord, and You, my God, I call:
Make me more and more believe Your promise,
Hope in You, and love You over all.

O memorial of my Savior dying,
Living Bread, that gives life to man;
Make my soul, its life from You supplying,
Taste Your sweetness, as on earth it can.

Deign, O Jesus, Pelican of heaven,
Me, a sinner, in Your Blood to lave,
To a single drop of which is given
All the world from all its sin to save.

Contemplating, Lord, Your hidden presence,
Grant me what I thirst for and implore,

In the revelation of Your essence
To behold Your glory evermore.

Follower:

Dear Saint, you are the most acclaimed intellectual genius in the Church even among non-Catholics, and you are known as the Patron of Schools.

Let all Christian teachers have a respect for truth no matter where they find it. Above all, let them learn through prayerful meditation on the written Word of God (Scripture) and on the life and conduct of Jesus Christ, the "Word of God" become Man.

✝   ✝   ✝

SAINT ELIZABETH OF PORTUGAL

Model Peacemaker and Religious in Spirit

1271-1336   Feast: July 4

Follower:

DEAR Saint, you were born in Spain and became Queen of Portugal but are best known as "the Peacemaker" because of your ability to bring about peace during your lifetime, even by dramatic battlefield interventions. You are also remembered for your aid to the poor and for leading a Religious life while living in the world.

Saint Elizabeth:

I must emphasize that God took good care of me. I was named after my great-aunt, Elizabeth of Hungary, who had been canonized seven years previously. My father was King Peter III of Aragon, and I was entrusted to my grandfather for my Christian upbringing, but he died before I was six years old.

With God's grace I was a devout and obedient child. Thus, at twelve years of age I consented to become the wife of Dionysius, King of Portugal. My husband was kind to me and never objected to my living the life of a Religious. God blessed us with two children.

Follower:

You showed extraordinary patience and gentleness that, thanks to the grace of God, enabled you to convert your husband from a life of immorality. Impressed by your outstanding charity toward the poor, he came to realize that he had a Saint in his house.

However, your charity was not mere humanitarianism, or the activity of a "social worker." You were animated by the Spirit of Christ, Who during His earthly life went about doing good.

Saint Elizabeth:

When we follow Christ, we must accept to bear the cross that He decides not to take away from us. My son, Alfonso, rebelled against his father, and my husband for a time suspected that I favored my son.

Follower:

Through your patient conduct, you were successful in bringing about the reconciliation between father and son. After your husband's death, you became a member of the Third Order of Saint Francis—for even as Queen you had recited not only the Divine Office but also the Offices of our Lady and of the Dead.

You also managed to reconcile your son, the King of Portugal, with your grandson, the King of Castile. But your self-sacrificing and strenuous efforts took their toll and you died shortly afterward. What a wonderful reception you must have been granted by the Prince of Peace Whom you had served and imitated so well!

Prayer of Saint Elizabeth

MARY, *Mother of grace,*
Mother of mercy,
shield us from the enemy
and receive us at the hour of death.

Follower:

Dear Saint, inspire us with a desire to accept and bear the cross that our Lord wants us to bear during our fleeting life upon earth.

May we always imitate your prayerful efforts to reconcile sinners with God and enemies with one another.

✛   ✛   ✛

SAINT CATHERINE OF SIENA

Exemplary Mystic and Doctor of the Church
1347-1380   Feast: Apr. 29

Follower:

DEAR Saint, you are one of the two women honored with the title of Doctor of the Church because of the treasury of spiritual writing found in your famous *Dialogues* and some 400 *Letters.* You also received the mark of our Lord's wounds on your body and, as it

SAINT CATHERINE OF SIENA: DIVINE PARADOX—
Mystic in tune with God and at the same time practical woman evolved in pressing everyday affairs, Saint Catherine has much to teach us. By God's grace, she was a Doctor though unlettered, a diplomat though unschooled, and a lover of God though untaught.

were, completed in your life the sufferings of Christ.

After a childhood made noteworthy by unusual spiritual gifts, you became a Dominican tertiary at eighteen and spent fully three years in prayer and solitude.

Saint Catherine:

I lived in very turbulent times, but I was fortunate to have God's light telling me what I had to do. Forty years before my birth the Popes had left Rome for Avignon—to the detriment of the Church.

I gathered about me a "spiritual family" of Priests, Nuns, and Laity, and we labored to deepen the spiritual life of leaders and people. In time I came to see that God wanted to make me a peacemaker and bring the Pope back to Rome.

Follower:

You had to overcome the might of France, the Sacred College, and the Papal household to convince the Pope (Gregory XI) to return to Rome. Yet with God's help you succeeded, thereby repelling the powers of evil that threatened to engulf the Church. And you went to your reward at the young age of thirty-three.

What a wonderful simplicity is found in a life like yours. You remained in union with God while being eminently practical in human affairs. Above all, you practiced much penance and constant prayer.

Saint Catherine:

I might point out that my life is a remarkable example of how God makes use of the lowly to bring about His purposes. I never learned to write and I knew no Latin (the language of the Church)—yet God deigned to work through me. It is clear that the teachings I professed were Divinely infused into my soul. Only with God's help did I dictate all my *Letters* and my *Dialogues*. His alone be the glory!

Prayer of Saint Catherine

W*HAT more could You give me than Yourself!*
You are the Fire that burns without consuming.
Your heat dissolves the soul's self-love
and takes away all cold.
Your brightness illumines me
and teaches me all Your truth.
You are the Light above all light
which supernaturally enlightens the eyes of my
    mind

and perfectly clarifies the light of faith,
that I may see that my soul is alive,
and in this light receive You—
the true Light!

Follower:

Dear Saint, simplicity is often absent in our modern society. People take pride in their self-reliance and independence (even from their Creator), and then they wonder why they are unsuccessful.

Make us walk in your footsteps, which are really those of our Lord. Teach us the simplicity of the children of God, which relies for all things on our Father in heaven.

✛   ✛   ✛

SAINT BERNARDINE

Promoter of Devotion to the Holy Name

1380-1444   Feast: May 20

Follower:

DEAR Saint, you are best remembered for your powerful preaching and for your unwearying promotion of devotion to the Holy Name of Jesus. While preaching you used to hold a board upon which were inscribed the first three letters of "Jesus" in its Greek form— IHS—surrounded by rays. And you continually urged the people to have devotion to that Holy Name.

Saint Bernardine:

Born in the Republic of Siena in 1380, I was orphaned at an early age. I was brought up and educated by a pious aunt, who loved me as if I were her own son.

In my youth, I joined the Confraternity of Our Lady and served the sick in the hospital. When the great pestilence broke out in 1400, I persuaded other young men to share these arduous duties. Then I entered the Fathers of the Strict Observance of the Order of Saint Francis.

Follower:

On becoming a priest in 1404, you devoted yourself to the office of preaching. For fourteen years your labors were confined to your own country, spreading devotion to the Holy Name of Jesus. Then you went on to become the Apostle of Italy in your time.

Saint Bernardine:

The acclaim that I received interfered with the work that I knew God wanted me to do. In

1427, I had to decline the Bishopric of Siena; in 1431, that of Ferrara; and again, in 1435, that of Urbino.

Follower:

The wondrous results of your sermons became a byward. However, you practiced the most sincere humility and always sought to conceal the talents God had given you.

In 1435, you were obliged to become vicar general of the Friars of the Strict Observance. You insisted upon instruction in theology and canon law as part of the regular curriculum. So well did you regulate this reform that it grew from 300 friars at your ordination to 4000 at your death.

Saint Bernardine:

In 1442, I received permission from the Pope to resign my office and return to what I regarded as my only vocation—preaching the Faith by my missionary journeys. Though my health was beginning to fail, I was able to continue the work of preaching in Romania, Ferrara, and Lombardy for two years.

Follower:

Then after giving a strenuous series of Lenten sermons on fifty consecutive days, you died on the way to Naples. The honor in which you were held by people is shown by the fact that you were canonized by Pope Nicholas V in 1450, only six years after your death.

Prayer of Saint Bernardine

O TRIUMPHANT Name,
O joy of angels and of the just,
O fear of hell:
in You
lies all hope of pardon, grace, and glory.
O most sweet Name,
You give pardon to sinners.

You renew us,
fill our hearts with Divine delight,
and cast out our fears.

O Name full of grace,
through You
Your faithful gain insight into great mysteries,
become aflame with Divine grace,
receive strength in their combats,
and are delivered from all evil.

Follower:

Dear Saint, we live in an age that accords little respect for any time-honored institution or custom. As a result, the respect once shown to the glorious Name of Jesus is in danger of being lost. That Name is constantly taken in vain.

Teach us to love and honor the Name of Jesus. Help us to realize that it is in that Name alone that we can be saved. Inspire us to invoke it religiously and promote devotion to it among our contemporaries.

✢   ✢   ✢

SAINT COLETTE

Inspired Religious and Spiritual Reformer

1381-1447   Feast: Mar. 6

Follower:

DEAR Saint, it is fashionable for men to speak about the "weaker sex" but in the spiritual order women often show themselves supremely powerful. This is admirably borne out in your life.

Born of humble and aged parents at Corbie, France, you seemed to have nothing to start with. Your parents died when you were twenty-two, and many must have thought that history would not even recall your name. Yet your life and your work will be remembered for ages to come.

Saint Colette:

Saint Francis of Assisi, whose life prompted me to become a Poor Clare, inspired me no doubt to begin by living as an anchoress—that is, to lead a solitary life—in accord with the Rule of the Franciscan Third Order.

Accordingly, I prayed much. I meditated on Holy Scripture. I lived and worked in loving intimacy with our Lord for four years. But in 1406 I realized that God desired that some people should live according to what we can call "the strict observance of Saint Clare."

Follower:

You received a wonderful favor. Pope Benedict XIII entrusted you with the task of reforming the Third Order. Bolstered by the knowledge that you were acting in harmony with God's will expressed by the Vicar of Christ, you traveled throughout France and parts of Belgium, particularly Flanders, reforming Poor Clare monasteries and founding others.

You saw to it that in such monasteries the original Rule was observed. Poor Clares lived, prayed, and practiced penance for God's glory and the spiritual good of souls.

Saint Colette:

I founded a monastery of Poor Clares at Ghent, East Flanders, and there my earthly life came to an end. It was also my good fortune on one of my journeys to encounter the saintly Joan of Arc, at Moulins in 1429.

What a simple, humble, and self-sacrificing young woman she turned out to be. Her motto was: "Let God be served first!" and she lived it to the full. For she loved her Crucified Savior "unto her own death" at the stake.

Follower:

You established fifteen communities and one of them still bears your name—"Colettines." You must have met many difficulties during your forty years of travels.

Saint Colette:

Yes—too numerous to mention. But I did not mind. Our Lord sustained me through the intercession of Mary, Francis, and Clare. We can do all things in Him Who strengthens us.

Prayer of Saint Colette

L ORD,
 teach me
Who You are
and who I am.

Follower:

Dear Saint, it has frequently happened that Religious changed their Rule contrary to the intention of their Founders out of the desire to be more up-to-date.

Bring about the reform of such Orders and Congregations. May they then receive numerous postulants who are animated by the Holy Spirit, as you were, instead of the spirit of secularism.

✛   ✛   ✛

SAINT RITA

Exemplary Wife and
Powerful Advocate
1381-1457   Feast: May 22

Follower :

DEAR Saint, you are the patroness of those in need, and for your lavishness in granting favors you have been called the Advocate of the "Hopeless" and even of the "Impossible."

You are so humble, so mortified, so patient, and so compassionate in love for your Crucified Jesus that you can obtain from Him even the most difficult of favors. Symbolic of this was the rose you requested when dying. Blooming in winter, it achieved the impossible!

Saint Rita:

You must remember always that it is God who achieves the impossible. Like His other servants, I am merely His instrument through whom He grants favors to human beings.

Perhaps I have more concern for those in desperate straits because my life seemed to be filled with problems. Married against my inclinations to a man of violent temper, I lived in terror for eighteen years. My only salvation lay in our Lord Who helped me grow in patience and accept—and even love—the cross that was mine.

Follower:

Your husband was then stabbed by an enemy. Helped by your kindness and prayers, he repented and died a good death. Shortly afterward your two sons also died.

You then joined the Community of Augustinian Nuns at Cascia in Umbria and became a model Religious, practicing charity toward all.

Saint Rita:

I had a great devotion to our Lord's Passion and often expressed the desire before a Crucifix to suffer for love of Him. One day one of the thorns fell from the Crucifix and left a deep wound in my forehead that refused to heal. For the rest of my life I suffered a pain similar to that of Jesus.

Follower:

You provide a good illustration of the accuracy of one of Saint Augustine's sayings: "Where there is love there is no suffering; and if there is suffering, suffering itself is loved."

Prayer of Saint Rita

O MY God and my Crucified Lord,
    You were innocent and without sin or crime,
yet You suffered so much for love of me!
You suffered arrest, buffeting, insults,
a scourging, a crown of thorns,
and finally a cruel death on the Cross.
Why do You wish that I—
Your unworthy servant who was the cause
of Your sufferings and Your pains—
should have no share in Your sufferings?

Follower:

Dear Saint, teach us that through the Cross of Christ heavenly grace is given us, our minds are strengthened, and we experience spiritual joy.

Help us to accept our own cross each day with sentiments similar to yours, and to follow our Crucified Lord through earthly sorrow to eternal happiness in heaven.

✠   ✠   ✠

SAINT FRANCES OF ROME

Model Wife and Exemplary Religious

1384-1440   Feast: Mar. 9

Follower:

DEAR Saint, you are one of the few women who combined the careers of model wife and exemplary Religious during their lifetime. Although born into a wealthy and noble family, you realized the lack of true value in earthly possessions and worldly honors.

At an early age, you learned to appreciate spiritual values because you took the Beatitudes seriously and loved to meditate on Christ—the Lord of heaven and earth Who chose to live as a poor Man and remain obedient to His creatures.

Saint Frances:

True, as a child, I had become acquainted with monasteries, and the life of cloistered Nuns attracted me. So I told my parents that I wanted to become a Religious. They did not agree with me, and I considered it proper to obey their wishes. At the age of thirteen I married a nobleman, Lawrence Ponziani.

Follower:

He must have been a good Christian inasmuch as he let you lead a very spiritual life. Of course, you also considered it obligatory to fulfill your domestic duties. We are told that in forty years of marriage you and your husband never had a quarrel.

A number of Roman ladies shared your ideal of a life of self-denial and good works "in the world," and you organized them into a society.

Saint Frances:

At one point during the Great Schism (which lasted from 1378 to 1417 and saw the sad bewildering spectacle of three claimants to the Papacy), my husband was banished and I had much to suffer. After the Schism he returned and recovered his estates.

However, worldly goods held no attraction for me. I had the greatest pleasure of being able to found an Oblate Congregation, and the Nuns accepted my suggestion that they should follow the Rule of Saint Benedict.

Follower:

After your husband's death, you joined that same Community in 1436 and became its director and model through your spirit of humility. The Lord gave you marvelous favors that helped you make progress in holiness. Pope Eugenius IV held you in great veneration and respected your advice.

Spiritual Words of Saint Frances

YOU must supply what is lacking in others. It is your vocation to pray and do penance for yourselves and for them.
You are the victims chosen to assuage
the wrath of God;
and your tears are the instrument
for extinguishing this conflagration [the Schism].

SAINT ANGELA MERICI: MODERN RELIGIOUS—
A woman of faith and vision, Saint Angela founded
a forward-looking Congregation to care for God's
people in a new age. Her example of selflessness
has attracted many followers and inspired countless others.

Follower:

Dear Saint, you lived during a time that was even more tumultuous than our own as far as religion was concerned. And you knew how to make people appreciate the Religious Life even in the cloister.

Teach us to realize that no time spent with God is ever wasted. Bring about a rebirth of genuine Religious Life where persons are truly consecrated to a life of intimate union with God and vicarious penance for sins.

✝   ✝   ✝

SAINT ANGELA MERICI

Astute Foundress and Dedicated Teacher

1474-1540   Feast: Jan. 7

Follower:

DEAR Saint, you were one of the first to grasp the changed role of women in the society transformed by the Renaissance. Your idea of a Religious Order without distinctive garb and without solemn vows and enclosure was also in advance of your time—although your Order was obliged to adopt the canonical safeguards then required of all Nuns.

Your Company of Saint Ursula (Ursulines) was the first teaching order of women. Much of the teaching took place in homes, for you hoped to effect an important change in social conditions. You rightly believed that disorder in society is the result of disorder in the family.

Saint Angela:

I was orphaned at ten and cared for by an uncle. At twenty, I joined the Third Order of Saint Francis and made my home into a small school for young girls. Through a vision God led me to found a religious community of teachers.

After founding a school in Brescia, I made a pilgrimage to the Holy Land and Rome, where Pope Clement VII was good enough to recognize my work.

Follower:

You renounced all your possessions so as to be freer to carry out your work. You also knew the value of lovingly receiving our Lord in Holy Communion, and your love for Him grew constantly. Inspired by the Spirit, you drew others to you to teach children for the sake of Christ.

Saint Angela:

Worldly people are very unhappy because they seek happiness where it cannot be found. Loving self-sacrifice for God's honor and Christlike charity toward those who are materially and spiritually poor is a source of true contentment.

People speak of Christ as the Man of Sorrows and Mary as the Mother of Sorrows, but both were the happiest human beings on earth because they led a holy and most loving, self-sacrificing life.

Follower:

That is why people should meditate on the life of Jesus and Mary and also on the lives of the Saints. It has been well said that a sad Saint is a sad sort of Saint—and really no Saint at all.

You, for example, loved to meditate on the Crucified Savior, but that did not make you gloomy. You often enjoyed an almost heavenly happiness.

Prayer of Saint Angela

M*Y Savior,
illumine the darkness of my heart,
and grant me the grace rather to die*

than to offend You again.
Guard my affections and my senses
that they may not stray in any direction.
Let me ever walk in the light of Your face,
the satisfaction of every afflicted heart.

Follower:

Dear Saint, in our day we are deluged with all kinds of teachers and constantly bombarded with instruction in living. Most of it, however, is given to gain selfish ends.

Teach us to follow your example of selfless instruction so that we may learn for ourselves and impart to others the Science of the Saints, the real science of living!

✜   ✜   ✜

SAINT THOMAS OF VILLANOVA

Outstanding Exemplar of Almsgiving

1486-1555   Feast: Sept. 22

Follower:

DEAR Saint, you are remembered for many things—ardent love for God, zeal for the promotion of studies and the missions of your Augustinian Order, and wholehearted service to the Church. Most of all, however, you are remembered as an Apostle of Charity and Almsgiving.

Taught by the example of your dedicated Christian parents, you could never resist giving alms from your boyhood onward. Your school lunch, clothes, shoes, and supplies from your parents' store—all were given away freely.

Saint Thomas:

You are right about the example of my parents. They taught me so well that all my life I had little regard for any kind of possessions but much concern for the welfare of others, especially their eternal welfare.

God was very good to me and gave me many graces, both internal and external—in the people I encountered, the things I did, and the circumstances of my life.

Follower:

Educated at the University of Alcala, you were a brilliant student and then became an outstanding Professor of Philosophy. But your primary interest was always in the Science of the Saints, the science of revealed teaching, and your life was always edifying.

Joining the Augustinian Order, you became a Priest, rose to be Provincial twice, and finally were made Archbishop of Valencia against your inclinations. All your life you strove for holiness and service to souls—becoming a veritable Apostle of Spain.

Saint Thomas:

Living as I did in a time when many were breaking away from the Church, I tried to keep my people faithful to her. She is the only one founded by our Lord and she brings Christ to the world through the Scriptures, the Liturgy, and her sacred Tradition.

Because of ill health I was unable to attend the Council of Trent but I was present at it in spirit through my brother Bishops and I endorsed what it decreed through the Holy Spirit.

Prayer of Saint Thomas of Villanova

LORD, *it is good for us to be here;*
do not let me descend from this height.
Your presence is enough for me;
do not, I beg You, leave me.
Let me spend my whole life here
and all my days.
What more could I desire?
It is this that I seek
and this alone that I ask.

Follower:

Dear Saint, in our day charity has become a part of government and big business. It has become organized and been converted into a religion-less philanthropy.

Teach us to turn this type of giving into a religious act. Make us give out of love for Christ and in union with Christ. Raise up selfless apostles of charity after your image.

✛   ✛   ✛

SAINT CAJETAN

Ecclesiastical Reformer and Religious Founder
1480-1547   Feast: Aug. 7

Follower:

Dear Saint, your life and work illumine the secret that Christ is found in His sick, and that they can best be cared for by those who love Christ and who pray unceasingly to Him.

You left few letters and no literary works, yet your influence on your time was great. You exhibited great holiness by your tirelessness in prayer and preaching, your Eucharistic devotion, your ascetic life, your unflagging charity, and your zealous ministry.

Saint Cajetan:

Through no merit of mine, God's grace was all around me. Born into a noble and Christian family of Vicenza, I studied law and could have followed a brilliant career in the Curia at Rome. But I felt like a fish out of water. I realized that I had a late vocation to the priesthood.

After ordination at thirty-six years of age, I formed a Religious Confraternity. Returning to Vicenza, I joined another Confraternity, and then went on to Venice to work among the sick and destitute.

Follower:

During this time the thought came to you to found a Religious Society of Priests whose members would take the evangelical vows. In conjunction with John Peter Caraffa, who later became Pope Paul IV, and two others you founded the Order of Clerks Regular (Theatines).

Saint Cajetan:

It was the intention of the founders that the members should devote themselves to preaching and to hospital work. Above all, they should lead the Laity back to the Sacraments and the Clergy back to an ordered life of prayer and study—with emphasis on the Liturgy.

Follower:

It is clear that you were working for a "reformation" within the Church rather than outside it as did the Protestant reformers in your day. At the same time, you did anything that would help the people's shockingly sad state, including establishing a pawnshop—run not for profit but for giving help to those in temporary difficulty.

Saint Cajetan:

God was unbelievably generous toward me. Why, then, should I not use my short life on earth to express my gratitude in striving for holiness and winning followers for Christ! After all, the Son of God Himself chose to become a Servant and to die in sacrifice for all.

Prayer of Saint Cajetan

S*UPREME Father,
aid the work of Your hand.
Help me to will nothing that You reject
and to reject nothing that You will.*

Follower:

Dear Saint, today there are some Catholics who act merely like "social workers" or humanists who do not even believe in God. Teach us to be true workers of charity for the sick and underprivileged.

Help us to obtain a spiritual renewal for all those with whom we come into contact each day—by our prayers and our example. In that way we will be doing our bit to renew the Church as well.

✛   ✛   ✛

SAINT JEROME EMILIANI

Religious Founder and Patron of Orphans

1486-1537   Feast: Feb. 8

Follower:

DEAR Saint, you went from a life of worldliness to a life of total concern for the welfare of orphans and abandoned children. So anxious were you about their spiritual well-being as well, that you were the first to teach such children our Holy Faith by means of set questions and answers.

You undoubtedly realized that for the unlettered this is the best system to receive and retain the truths of Faith.

Saint Jerome:

In my youthful exuberance and chase after vanities, I became a Venetian soldier and took part in a local war. I was taken prisoner and through Mary's special intervention set free. I then began a new kind of life, a total Christian life, Christ-centered and expressing itself in compassion.

Our Lord showed concern for children and said: "Let the children come to Me" (Mt 19:14). Yet there are still very many children who are materially poor. And how many others are spiritually deprived and neglected! Yet think of all the money that is spent and all the energy that is expended on luxuries, entertainments, and frivolous pursuits!

Follower:

You were ordained a Priest when you reached the age of thirty-seven. But then without delay you threw yourself fully into the work that is connected with your name. You established the very first orphanage and then many others, as well as a hospital and a house for fallen women.

Saint Jerome:

When God wants you to do something, you can count on receiving whatever you need to get the work done. After a while I considered it important to obtain full-time cooperators who were also Religious. So I founded the Congregation of Clerics Regular of Somascha.

Follower:

You died as you had learned to live. There was an epidemic and naturally you were ministering to the sick. You too became a victim of the plague, and while transporting a victim to a place of burial you yourself died.

Prayer of Saint Jerome

D EAREST *Jesus,*
    be to me
not a Judge
but a Savior.

Follower:

Dear Saint, you know that even in our age, which prides itself on being enlightened, many children are still abused and abandoned, subjected to abominable living conditions and given intolerable bad example.

Pray that parents may recognize their privilege of bringing up "children of God" who should become followers of Jesus, Son of God and Son of Mary.

✝   ✝   ✝

SAINT PHILIP NERI

Model of Cheerful Holiness

1515-1595   Feast: May 26

Follower :

DEAR Saint, you must have been a delightful person to know because you were a *cheerful* Christian. You attracted people to you by a good-hearted temperament, by beautiful liturgical services, and by turning your living quarters into a "home of Christian mirth."

You lived as a layman until the age of thirty-five—tutoring, writing poetry, and studying philosophy and theology. Hence you concentrated on encouraging the Laity to strive for perfection just as much as the Religious do.

Saint Philip:

I had learned from my devout Florentine parents and my teachers of theology to place

SAINT PHILIP NERI: CHEERFUL CHRISTIAN—A highly cultured and indefatigable worker, Saint Philip was the very image of the cheerful Christian. He attracted multitudes to him and taught them the true sense of God.

great confidence in prayer. So I fully appreciated the power of cloistered prayer.

However, with God's help, I came to realize that in my era of turbulent change there was urgent need to go out to the people in their everyday surroundings. We needed Priests and Brothers who could be in closer contact with people living in the world—after the manner of Christ Himself and the Apostles.

Follower:

The Holy Spirit worked powerfully in you and you followed His inspirations. You founded a Confraternity in honor of the Holy Trinity whose members would serve pilgrims and sick people. A little later, you experienced an ecstasy of Divine Love that left a permanent physical effect on your heart.

After being ordained in 1551, you gathered around yourself men who were called Oratorians, with headquarters at a new Church of La Vallicella donated by Pope Gregory XIII. It is still called the New Church.

Saint Philip:

Remember that it was God Who made me mirthful and attractive to others. I merely cooperated with His grace and strove to help the young men of Rome. Our Oratory became a center of glorious worship of God, of reconciliation of sinners, and a powerful broadcasting station of spiritual enlightenment and charitable service of the poor.

Follower:

Countless are the Religious, Priests, and Laity who have been inspired by you who were yourself a transmitter of the Holy Spirit. You remain a model by your humility, charity, and fidelity.

Prayer of Saint Philip Neri

M*Y Lord Jesus,*
I want to love You
but You cannot trust me.
If You do not help me,
I will never do any good.
I do not know You;
I look for You but I do not find You.
Come to me, O Lord.
If I knew You,
I would also know myself.
If I have never loved You before,
I want to love You truly now.
I want to do Your will alone;
putting no trust in myself,

I hope in You,
O Lord.

Follower:

Dear Saint, I am sure you have realized that our times bear more than a cursory resemblance to yours. Teach us how to remain faithful in spite of the storms around us.

Obtain also for us a disposition of Christian cheerfulness and good humor. Make us bring natural and supernatural sunshine into our lives and those of others—for we bear within us the Sun of Justice, Jesus the Lord!

✢   ✢   ✢

SAINT JOHN OF THE CROSS

Outstanding Mystical Writer and Doctor

1542-1591   Feast: Dec. 14

Follower:

DEAR Saint, you are more renowned for your mystical writings than for your life. Even non-Christians are attracted by your literary prowess and your deep spirituality.

Your holiness shines through every page of your writings. One of your guiding principles was: "Live in the world as if only God and your soul were in it; then your heart will never be made captive by any earthly thing."

Saint John:

Actually—as you know—I attained no renown during life but only after death. And the secret of my spiritual success is the grace of God and devout parents. From them I learned the special devotion to the Crucified Lord and His Mother that helped me throughout life.

Follower:

We also know your great love for the compassionate Savior Who so greatly loved the poor, which you showed even as a youth by serving the ailing poor in a hospice.

After your studies, you became a Carmelite and practiced great austerities, inspired by the all-holy One Who died on the Cross for sinners.

Saint John:

Shortly after being ordained a Priest I had the great privilege of meeting the extraordinary Saint Teresa of Avila, who was some thirty years older than I.

Although she sought my help in her reform movement, it was she who inspired me both for my own sanctification and for the reform of the Carmelites.

Follower:

You were the first member of the Reformed Order of Carmelite Friars. You were engaged in many works as superior, prior, and vicar general, but you managed to remain always in loving union with your Divine Master.

You also suffered much at the hands of some of your more irascible brothers in religion. But through it all you remained imperturbable and forgiving.

Saint John:

My conduct was guided by Christ on the Cross. It was only fitting that I should carry my little cross in union with Him. Christ overshadowed the world with love and compassion—and it was through the Cross that He did so. I felt that I as His follower should do likewise.

Prayer of Saint John of the Cross

M Y God,
You still will not take away
what You have given me
in Your only Son, Jesus Christ.
In Him, You have given me all that I desire.
You will, therefore, no longer delay—
and this is my joy—
provided that I wait for You.

Mine are the heavens,
mine is the earth and mine are the peoples;
mine are the just and mine are the sinners;
mine are the angels;
mine is the mother of God—
God Himself is mine, for me—
for mine is Christ
and everything is for me.

Follower:

Dear Saint, self-renunciation and love of the Cross are the hallmarks of your spirituality. They are two characteristics that are foreign to the modern mentality.

Teach us to cultivate these two traits in our lives and to move others to do likewise so that we may spread the knowledge and love of the Crucified to our contemporaries.

✝   ✝   ✝

SAINT STANISLAUS KOSTKA

Model of Fidelity
to a Religious Rule

1550-1568   Feast: Aug. 15

Follower:

DEAR Saint, the remarkable fact about you is that in the short span of eighteen years you became so respected—although your outward life was uneventful by human standards —as to be canonized within forty years after your death.

You showed outstanding fortitude and generosity in standing up to the misguided attempts of your father to prevent you from becoming a Jesuit, and you exhibited unflinching obedience to a Religious Rule of life. Indeed, you always carried your own handwritten copy upon your heart and you followed its provisions in minute detail.

Saint Stanislaus:

Born in Poland, I had the great blessing of being brought up in a truly Christian way in which discipline was connected with true love. This, together with God's grace, made me willing and even anxious to bear unpleasant things for God. A brother of mine disliked and harassed me for two years, and my father, a powerful nobleman, ridiculed my vocation to be a Jesuit.

Follower:

You had a great devotion to our Lady, we are told, and the good fortune to receive spiritual direction from saintly Jesuits. Too bad that today many do not want spiritual directors, and some end up by doing "their own thing" which is not in accord with God's intentions.

Saint Stanislaus:

You are right. God often uses inspiring instruments that we must accept in order to follow properly the particular vocation He had in mind for us from all eternity. I received the grace of seeing Mary with the Holy Child.

I first studied with the Jesuits in Vienna and decided to join their Society. Trying to prevent being called home, I journeyed in disguise 350 miles on foot to Germany where I met Saint Peter Canisius who gave me shelter for three weeks and then made arrangements for me to go to Rome.

Follower:

There you entered the Saint Andrew Novitiate, accepted by Saint Francis Borgia who later became the third Superior General of the Order.

For ten months you led such an exemplary life as a novice that you have been named the Patron of Novices. Most of all, you were outstanding for your profound love and devotion toward Jesus in the Blessed Sacrament and His holy Mother.

Prayer of Saint Stanislaus Kostka

MY loving Mother,
I dedicate to you my work,
my efforts,
my spirit,
and my heart.
Kindly accept this small gift
offered out of reverence and love for you.
Please offer it in turn
to Christ your Son,
my Redeemer.

Follower:

Dear Saint, our youth today seem to have as their motto: "Let us eat, drink, and be mer-

SAINT CAMILLUS DE LELLIS: GOOD SAMARITAN
—A huge man with an even greater love for Christ, Saint Camillus revolutionized the care of the sick. He was the forerunner of all who see Christ in the sick and render unstinting service to them.

ry, for tomorrow we shall die." And they thus fail—once upon eternity—to make the necessary preparations and investments for the blessed life with God and the Saints.

Teach them to follow your inspiration. Show them how to harness their energies and use them for their own and others' spiritual fulfillment—and so give glory to God.

✣   ✣   ✣

SAINT CAMILLUS DE LELLIS

Good Samaritan and Patron of Hospitals

1550-1614   Feast: July 14

Follower:

DEAR Saint, you are sometimes called the Red Cross Saint because the members of your Congregation wear a black habit with a red cross on their breast but even more because you helped revolutionize the care of the sick.

You were an innovator in the field of health and are credited with introducing open windows in hospitals, medical dieting, and isolation of contagious cases. Above all, you honored the sick as living images of Christ, and saw service to them as service to Christ.

Saint Camillus:

Remember one thing, however. Although I was big in body (six feet six inches high and broad in shoulder), I was small in mind. I entered the Venetian army at seventeen and for eight years afterward was a soldier of fortune with an overpowering impulse to gamble, which kept me in constant trouble.

Through the grace of God, I came in touch with the Capuchins of Abruzzi and became converted to Christ. I wanted to join their Order, but God wanted otherwise and gave me an ulcerous leg that barred my being accepted.

Follower:

You finally went to a Hospital of Incurables in Rome and in time became its administrator. The Lord made you look upon yourself more and more as a servant of the sick, and you even learned to render the most unpleasant and humiliating services to those poor sufferers. You saw at first hand the shocking state of the hospitals and the gross inadequacy of the nursing staff.

Saint Camillus:

That is a true picture, and it made me want to help. At the age of thirty-two I began to learn grammar with children, for I was still il-literate.

I learned well enough to be able to be ordained, and then with God's help I laid the foundation for what came to be called "The Congregation of Clerics Regular," whose members would take care of the sick.

Follower:

I know that you had to overcome many obstacles but you had the advantage of having Saint Philip Neri as your spiritual director. And you inspired all by serving and consoling and praying with the patients day and night.

Prayer of Saint Camillus de Lellis

O LORD,
save Your servant
whom You have redeemed
by Your Precious Blood.

Follower:

Dear Saint, there is still much room in our day for showing compassion to the sick. Inspire all who serve the sick (doctors, nurses, volunteers) to do so not only with the proper care for their patients but also with the proper attitude within themselves.

Let them ever keep in mind the example set forth by our Lord in His parable of the Good Samaritan, who not only took care of the wounded man but did so unselfishly and at his own expense. Indeed, let us all learn to see Christ in the sick and to serve Him without reserve.

✝   ✝   ✝

SAINT MARGARET CLITHEROW

Exemplary Wife, Mother, and Martyr
1555-1586   Feast: Mar. 26

Follower:

DEAR Saint, your short life is an apt illustration of three basic Christian attitudes: the search for Truth (God), the joyful embrace of that Truth, and the selfless professing of that Truth even in giving one's life if need be.

For you knew that no matter what people may have to suffer on earth it is insignificant in comparison with what God has destined for those who die in the Lord.

Saint Margaret:

I was born at Middleton, England, of Protestant parents, but I came to realize with

God's help that I should belong to the one true Church.

God had given me a joyful temperament and I liked to repeat what the Liturgy loves to say in Advent and Lent: "Rejoice in the Lord." For our Lord was certainly the most joyful Man who ever lived.

Follower:

We know that you had good looks, that you were always ready for a laugh, and that you were full of wit and merriment. You became the devoted wife of John Clitherow, a well-to-do butcher, and a loving mother of two children.

After embracing the Catholic Faith, you showed great courage in hiding and harboring fugitive Priests so that they could keep the Faith alive amid widespread anti-Catholic feeling.

Saint Margaret:

For my efforts, I was thrown into jail and subjected to treatment calculated to force me to renounce my Faith. The persecutors were clever, alternatingly gentle and severe. But by the grace of God I did not yield.

Follower:

When you learned that you were condemned to be crushed to death, you said: "My flesh is troubled but my spirit greatly rejoices. For the love of God pray for me, and ask all good people to do likewise." When you were led to the place of execution, all marveled at your joyful, smiling countenance—such was your desire for God!

Saint Margaret:

During the execution that took about fifteen minutes, all my bones were broken. I prayed as long as I was conscious—trusting that the Lord would help me bear it—and He did.

Prayer of Saint Margaret Clitherow

I PRAY for the Catholic Church,
   for the holiness of the Pope,
for the Cardinals,
for all who have care of souls,
and for all Christian princes in the world.

Follower:

Dear Saint, the world today is in dire need of souls who will stand up for their convictions and at the same time will present a joyous countenance to all.

Grant us courage and good humor so that we may profess our Faith joyfully in the Catholic Church that was founded by the Savior of the world.

✝   ✝   ✝

SAINT FRANCIS CARACCIOLO

Religious Founder and Devotee
of the Blessed Sacrament

1563-1608   Feast: June 4

Follower:

DEAR Saint, you are a perfect example of how God makes His will known to us by means of seeming misfortunes and apparent accidents as well as the daily circumstances of life. You knew how to read the signs of God everywhere.

You were also the originator of Perpetual Adoration of the Blessed Sacrament by stipulating in your Rule that members of the Congregation spend an hour a day before the Blessed Sacrament in rotation.

Saint Francis:

You are right. A mistaken diagnosis of leprosy and imminent death changed the course of my life in the Kingdom of Naples. I vowed to work for God if spared, and on getting well I became a Priest, working with prisoners and condemned criminals.

Then a chance reception of a letter addressed to a relative who had the same first name (Ascanio) put me in touch with the persons who became cofounders with me of the Congregation of Regular Clerics Minor.

Follower:

It was on the occasion of your Religious Profession that you chose to be called Francis. Two years later you became the Superior of the Congregation and then traveled especially in Spain where you established several Religious Houses.

You suffered many great hardships. But like your patron, Francis of Assisi, you rejoiced because you were thus walking in the steps of your Divine Master, Who chose to live in poverty.

Saint Francis:

Meditating on the sufferings of our Crucified Lord is a source of great inspiration for us, and I learned to live not only in the spirit of poverty but in actual poverty.

In Rome I lived in a hospice for poor people and associated with a leper. Association with suffering people becomes a spiritual exercise and is a source of great joy, when we learn to see Christ in them.

Prayer of Saint Francis Caracciolo

*L**ET us go!
Let us go!*
To heaven!

Follower:

Dear Saint, you died at a relatively early age (forty-four) but you had done much. Teach us to see the signs of God in every event of life.

Instill in us a love for Jesus in the Blessed Sacrament and help us to see Him in our neighbor, especially the poorest of all. Pray that we may be inspired by your spirit and therefore also by the Holy Spirit, "Father of the poor."

✝   ✝   ✝

SAINT MARY MAGDALENE DE PAZZI

Mystic, Ecstatic, and Faithful Religious

1566-1607   Feast: May 25

Follower:

DEAR Saint, your wonderful vocation as a mystic and ecstatic is far removed from the lives of most Catholics. We find it hard to imagine what such a life is like. Yet we know that it is such lives that provide tremendous spiritual power for the world.

Your life bears eloquent witness to the oft-repeated phrase that God works in strange ways. It is now very clear that you were given Divine knowledge and anticipated many of the most modern directions taken by the Church in the fields of the Trinity, Christology, the Eucharist, Ecclesiology, and Liturgy.

Saint Mary:

You must understand that although my vocation was different from the more usual ones, it was still a vocation to which I was drawn by God's grace. Seen from the outside, the life of a mystic and ecstatic appears otherworldly and completely unappealing. But it is a life of profound union with God and gives great peace in spite of sufferings and trials of every kind.

Follower:

Yours was truly a Divine vocation. At the age of twelve you took a vow of perpetual virginity although you were from a noble Florentine family. Shortly afterward you entered the Carmelite Order, choosing a particular convent because you would be able to receive Holy Communion frequently there.

You became a model of true holiness for all who knew you. You were always ready to sit up at night to comfort the sick, and during the day you joyfully assisted anyone who needed your help.

Saint Mary:

Out of obedience to my superiors I set down in writing all the revelations and visions that God deigned to send me. They may thus be of help to Christians of all ages. I say this with no trace of vanity or pride, for we do not experience such things here.

Follower:

You also had a famous saying: "Either let me suffer or let me die." Your Divine Bridegroom permitted you to suffer greatly during a protracted illness, but He then took you to heaven at the age of forty-one.

Saint Mary:

You also mentioned serving others. Already on earth this is a source of joy: to help and encourage the afflicted to return good for evil. Did not our Lord do this perfectly? And how true also are His words recalled for us by Saint Paul: "There is greater happiness in giving than in receiving" (Acts 20:35). Then at our death He will add for us an unbelievably generous "reward."

Prayer of Saint Mary Magdalene de Pazzi

Y*OUR Providence, O Lord, is so great*
that You take care of all Your creatures
as if there were only one,
and You take care of each one
as if all others were enclosed in it.
If people could only understand and recognize
Your all-embracing Providence
and that they can unite with an all-providing
     God,
how different would be
their ideas of earthly values!
Grant us absolute confidence in You,
most Merciful God!

Follower:

Dear Saint, you know how much selfishness there is today. We greatly need your example. In you we should see one proof of the fact that "the charity of God is poured into our hearts by the Holy Spirit Who has been given to us" (Rom 5:5).

Ask the Holy Spirit to give us a new Pentecost, making Christians more Christlike, more self-sacrificing, in imitation of the One Who chose to die for sinful and ungrateful human beings.

✣　　✣　　✣

SAINT FRANCIS DE SALES

Outstanding Doctor of the Spiritual Life
1567-1622   Feast: Jan. 24

Follower:

DEAR Saint, you are best known for your practice of the virtue of meekness and for your sound advice for the spiritual life. You were a Christian humanist, adapting the genuine good of the Renaissance to the Christian way of life.

Your classic book *Introduction to the Devout Life* shows how all Christians can live their Faith *in the world* and attain true devo-

SAINT FRANCIS DE SALES: INSPIRED WRITER—
A man of true Christian meekness, Saint Francis
helped the laity to live a Christian life in the world. He
gave a wealth of common-sense advice—always
solidly grounded on the teachings of the Church.

tion. It is filled with common sense in applying truly Catholic principles.

Saint Francis:

I was fortunate in being born to a devout Catholic family and receiving a good religious education. By the time I graduated with degrees in law and theology I knew I was called to the Priesthood.

Armed with love for Christ and His teaching, I tried to practice Christlike meekness and patience as I sought to bring back many Calvinists to the true Faith. For I believed that "we can catch more flies with a spoonful of honey than with barrels of vinegar."

Follower:

After you were made Bishop of Geneva, you continued your self-sacrificing work and manifested your love for Mary by founding the Congregation of the Visitation Sisters of Our Lady.

As our Lord loved Martha and Mary, so did you have a spiritual friendship with Sister Jane Frances de Chantal.

Saint Francis:

You have clearly recalled some facts regarding my life and works. You did not mention how for many years I fought against the tendency to yield to anger, Also, of course, it was by the grace of God that I was able to do some good.

I have come to realize how extremely kind God is toward those who totally *abandon themselves* to His Fatherly love. When we thus give up everything, God takes up everything and guides us in all things.

Prayer of Saint Francis de Sales

O GOD,
I vow and consecrate to You
all that is in me:
my memory and my actions
to God the Father;
my understanding and my words
to God the Son;
my will and my thoughts
to God the Holy Spirit;
my heart and my body,
my tongue, my senses, and all my sorrows
to the Sacred Humanity of Jesus Christ,
Who was content to be betrayed
into the hands of wicked men
and to suffer the torment of the Cross.

Follower:

Dear Saint, we have great need today of your virtues and your spiritual advice. There is so much self-reliance and so much anger and violence toward one another.

Teach us to put our trust in God and practice the virtue of meekness toward others. Help us to call upon Mary our Advocate with the same devotion that you did throughout life.

✣   ✣   ✣

SAINT ALOYSIUS GONZAGA

Self-Sacrificing Youth
and Exemplary Novice

1568-1591   Feast: June 21

Follower:

DEAR Saint, your life-situation was far above that of most Catholics and can scarcely be imagined by us. Your family (Gonzaga) was related to half the rulers of Europe in your time, and you could have inherited all their pomp and power. Instead it repelled you.

Devoted to Christ and to His truth, you gave up your inheritance. You are thus the epitome of Christian manhood—clearheaded, unbribable, and completely selfless. Only your strength of character enabled you to overcome the host of worldly traditions that sought to draw you into a vain existence.

Saint Aloysius:

I realized that the society into which I was born could not be reformed from within. I sought to reform it through my membership in the Society of Jesus where I could practice poverty and chastity without being deluged with ecclesiastical dignities of all kinds.

My dear mother soothed my father's anger over the loss of a favored son to religion, and I joined the Society at the age of seventeen as a novice. I was fortunate to have as my spiritual director the saintly and learned Robert Bellarmine who helped me advance, with God's grace, in the spiritual life.

Follower:

What has always stood out in your short life is your love of chastity coupled with heroic penance and assiduous prayer. This makes you an excellent model for youth—but only if you are presented as you really were rather than as some cardboard figure without life.

Saint Aloysius:

Indeed, I was all too human. Without God's grace I could never have kept from sinning grievously. What drew me to the Jesuits was their happy blend of a Religious life and a ministry in the world.

I was most happy during a severe plague in 1591 to be permitted to serve the sick in a hospital opened by the Jesuits. I came to realize how true are Christ's words: "There is greater happiness in giving than in receiving" (Acts 20:35).

Follower:

You never minded what people said about you. Your great desire was to follow the Divine Master Who chose to be crucified for us. You showed love for critics and enemies and strove to follow the inspirations of the Spirit.

You also had great devotion to Mary the Virgin Mother of God. She became your Mother in the spiritual life.

Prayer of Saint Aloysius Gonzaga

O HOLY Mary,
   my Lady,
*into your blessed trust and safekeeping
and into the depths of your mercy*

*I commend my soul and body
this day,
every day of my life,
and at the hour of my death.*

*To you I entrust
all my hopes and consolations,
all my trials and miseries,
my life and the end of my life.
By your most holy intercession
and by your merits,
may all my actions be directed and disposed
according to your will
and the Will of your Divine Son.*

Follower:

Dear Saint, you know how badly our youth need real heroes. They are continually subjected to false leaders and false values.

Teach them to follow you in strength of character, purity, and love for God and fellow humans. Inspire some of them to join the Religious way of life and remain ever faithful to it

✢   ✢   ✢

SAINT VINCENT DE PAUL

Outstanding Exemplar
of Charity

1581-1660   Feast: Sept. 27

Follower:

DEAR Saint, the mere mention of your name suggests a litany of virtues: humility, zeal, mercy, self-sacrifice. It also recalls your many foundations: Works of mercy, Congregations, Societies. Most of all, it suggests a towering figure in the history of charitable enterprises.

Born of a poor family materially speaking, you were rich spiritually, endowed by your parents with great love for God and for neighbor. This spiritual wealth made you profligate in dispensing all worldly possessions to the poor.

Saint Vincent:

Material poverty is not necessarily an obstacle to a truly Christian life, though it may at times have prevented some from reaching the priesthood. God was kind to me, however. Franciscans, followers of the Poor Man of Assisi, gave me my first schooling, and a generous gentleman enabled me to continue my studies; so there was no additional burden for my parents. I studied theology at Toulouse, and it was in that city that I was ordained a priest at the early age of twenty.

Follower:

We are told that at a later time you met with great dangers. You fell into the hands of African pirates and were treated as a slave for almost two years. But God wanted you for a special ministry and enabled you to escape.

Passing through Rome, you returned to France. For some time, you taught the children of the Count de Joigny who was general of the galleys of France.

Saint Vincent:

I was overjoyed when I was able to preach missions and lay the foundations for the Society of the Mission or Lazarists as well as the Sisters of Charity. Our sole intention was to help people.

Follower:

You are clearly an outstanding symbol of charity, a charity toward all classes of people but principally the poor, the neglected and abandoned. Though extremely active in all those works of charity, you still managed to remain prayerful, to live in constant union with Jesus. You did not become a mere social worker who forgets the God Who is Love.

Saint Vincent:

You are right in speaking of the danger of over-activity, which is often an occasion for neglecting prayer. Faith without works is dead, but work without prayerfulness can lead to spiritual death.

Prayer of Saint Vincent de Paul

O GOD,
we give ourselves to You
for the rest of our lives
in order to serve our masters—the poor.
We ask this grace of You
by Your love for us.

Follower:

Dear Saint, you know that in our day there are many people involved in organized charity. Grant that they may truly love those whom they care for.

Help us to imitate you and like you be animated by the Holy Spirit to provide for the spiritual or material needs of others, especially the disadvantaged. Above all, let us do so out of love for Christ.

✤   ✤   ✤

SAINT JOHN BERCHMANS

Model of Simplicity and Obedience

1599-1621   Feast: Nov. 20

Follower:

DEAR Saint, the simplicity and single-mindedness of your life are evident in the words you uttered on your deathbed. Clasping your Crucifix, your Rosary, and your Religious Rule, you exclaimed: "These are my three treasures. With these I will gladly die."

You thus showed how a deep love for Christ, Mary, and your Religious vocation enabled you to attain sanctity by your fidelity in the everyday duties of your Religious and student life.

Saint John:

God was good and brought me into a family of devout Catholics. After my mother's death, my father became a Priest and two of my brothers and sisters became Religious.

I grew up with the idea that God's will was manifested to me in the legitimate commands of parents and superiors. And I combined the external obedience to these with submission to the interior guidance of the Holy Spirit.

Follower:

The Holy Spirit (and probably Saint Ignatius) prompted you to continue your studies in Mechlin where the Jesuits had established a new college. At the age of eighteen, you traveled to Rome on foot for further studies.

Your teachers regarded you as very talented. After three years of impeccable conduct as a scholastic, you were asked to engage in a public debate. But you were stricken from an undiagnosed sickness and were called to heaven at the age of twenty-one.

Saint John:

I was always devoted to Jesus the Priest-Victim Whose sacrifice on the Cross is not merely remembered but, as it were, broadcast in a living manner in the Mass. I also spent much time in adoration before Jesus in the Blessed Sacrament.

Follower:

There is a captivating simplicity about your holy life. You did well any work entrusted to you, and you did it for God's glory and the sanctification of souls.

Saint John:

Simplicity is the mark of Christ's teaching and practice. How simple and understandable is the "Our Father" that He gave us. It tells us that God is our infinitely loving Father and we must honor Him, work for the establishment of His Reign in us, and always do what is His will. We must pray for our needs of body and soul, and forgive those who have offended us.

Follower:

You are saying that Jesus teaches us our fundamental obligations by the words of that prayer, which give honor to God and at the same time ask for His help.

Prayer of Saint John Berchmans

MY Lord,
    You know that You are all I ever had,
and all I have now in this life.
Do not abandon me,
my Lord Jesus.

Follower:

Dear Saint, you know that in our day obedience has become something of a forgotten virtue. Everyone emphasizes doing one's own thing.

Teach us how to reconcile this desire for self-fulfillment with obedience to God's will. Make us truly know ourselves so that we can give wholehearted obedience to the vocation that God has given each of us, which will result in our truest and most legitimate fulfillment.

✠   ✠   ✠

SAINT MARGARET MARY ALACOQUE

Apostle of Devotion to the Sacred Heart

1647-1690   Feast: Oct. 16

Follower:

DEAR Saint, it was to you especially that our Divine Lord revealed His wish that His Sacred Heart (a symbol of His burning love for human beings) should be honored not only on a feast but frequently; and great promises were made to those who practiced that devotion.

SAINT MARGARET MARY: DEVOTEE OF THE SACRED HEART—An unlettered Religious, Saint Margaret Mary Alacoque had a surpassing love for the Sacred Heart of Jesus. Favored with visions of that Heart, she became the prime mover in the modern restoration of that devotion in the Church.

By this devotion God wanted to remind human beings of the enormous love He has for His creatures and the self-sacrificing love Jesus has toward each of us. Such love calls in turn for a response of love on our part.

Saint Margaret:

I was an uneducated girl. But I had a devotion to the Heart of Jesus from my youth, and I had resolved to give myself totally to Jesus, my Heavenly Bridegroom.

Hearing about the Visitandine Nuns, founded by the wonderful Francis de Sales, I quite naturally asked them to accept me into their Order.

Follower:

We know that you had many sufferings. It seems almost natural that apostles of some great Christian cause should suffer much—from illness or contradictions or both. Saint Teresa of Avila said that the Divine Lord did not spare His servants.

We cannot imagine a more loving Bridegroom than Christ, yet He often lets His "Brides" suffer very much and sometimes for long periods.

Saint Margaret Mary:

I must point out, however, that Jesus always gives us the means whereby to bear that suffering with equanimity. For example, He gave me a good spiritual director, Blessed Claude de la Colombiere, who was my support.

I learned to be patient in suffering, and even to welcome it because I felt closer to the Savior Who freely chose to suffer so much for me.

Follower:

What you are saying is that our devotion to the Sacred Heart should not consist in using it as a sort of elevator that brings us safely to heaven. We should love the Sacred Heart *unconditionally* for the greater glory of God and the good of souls.

Saint Margaret Mary:

A "go-getting" devotion is not a religious devotion. True Christian devotion is a "giving" devotion. All the Saints have seen this point and have regulated their lives accordingly.

Prayer of Saint Margaret Mary

I, N . . ., *give myself
to the Sacred Heart of our Lord Jesus Christ,*

and I consecrate to Him
my person and my life,
my actions, pains, and sufferings,
so that henceforth I shall be unwilling
to make use of any part of my being
except for the honor, love, and glory
of the Sacred Heart.

Follower:

Dear Saint, the modern idea is to flee suffering at any cost. There is such an accent on well-being that people cannot tolerate the thought of being incapacitated in any way.

Teach us to have a Christian attitude toward suffering and to bear it in union with Jesus Who bore so much for us. Let us entrust ourselves to the Sacred Heart in sickness or in health and in all the circumstances of life.

✢   ✢   ✢

SAINT VERONICA GIULIANI

Follower of the Crucified

1660-1727   Feast: July 9

Follower:

DEAR Saint, you are one of a few souls privileged to share the very sufferings of our

Lord in His Passion—the Stigmata. At the same time, your case is an outstanding one in the history of mystical phenomena, for we have meticulous records of it kept under the watchful care of your Religious Superiors.

Spiritual theologians can thus examine your life and sufferings in detail. This will contribute to more knowledge of the entire field of Stigmata in the Church and be of help to the spiritual life of all Catholics by the conclusions drawn.

Saint Veronica:

Already at an early age as a member of a well-to-do Italian family, I had great devotion to Jesus Crucified. I had heard of Saint Francis of Assisi who received the Stigmata, so well expressing his desire to resemble Christ in His sufferings.

Accordingly, I was very happy when I was permitted to enter the novitiate of the strict Order of Poor Clares founded by Saint Francis in union with Saint Clare.

Follower:

As you well know, the Church is never eager to accept Stigmatization as a fact. We are not told that you received the Stigmata but it is reported that you had a vision of Jesus bearing His Cross and later another vision in which you were offered the cup of Christ's sufferings —which you accepted.

Saint Veronica:

I had no desire to receive the Stigmata nor did I pray to have visions of our Lord. After all, Mary did not have the Stigmata yet she underwent so much suffering during our Lord's Passion.

I quickly learned as a Poor Clare how great is the value of obedience to lawful authority. A disobedient Religious is a contradiction in terms.

Follower:

In spite of your deeply mystical bent, you were also steeped in common sense as well as humble obedience. Hence, it is not surprising that you remained novice-mistress for twenty-four years. Because the Nuns had much confidence in you, they made you Abbess for eleven years.

Saint Veronica:

Perhaps the good influence I exerted on postulants, novices, and the community as a whole was the result of my enthusiasm for the Religious Life in which we bind ourselves to the Divine Bridegroom. Animated by the Holy Spirit, I could not help stressing the need for humility, obedience, and an all-embracing love.

Prayer of Saint Veronica Giuliani

O MY God,
  inflame my heart,
consume me in the fire of Your love.
O infinite Love of my Savior, come to me
that I may love You with Your own love.
Come quickly, O Love,
O Love of my God!

Follower:

Dear Saint, you combined a deep mystical life with a meticulous practical life. Teach us how to remain united with God amid the most pressing tasks of everyday existence.

Help us to bear our crosses with resignation and to remain unwavering in our love for our God Who is Love Itself.

✜   ✜   ✜

SAINT PAUL OF THE CROSS

Religious Founder and Mystic

1694-1775   Feast: Oct. 19

Follower:

DEAR Saint, your very name is an inspiration to us. It reminds us of the great convert Saint Paul who said: "I wish to know nothing but Christ and Him Crucified."

We also recall the Divine promise to Constantine: "In this Sign [the Cross] you will conquer." But this is especially true when we want to be victorious in our battle against the diabolical enemy of our soul. And did not Christ proclaim: "When I am lifted up [on the Cross], I will draw all things to Myself!" (Jn 12:32).

Saint Paul:

You are right. Who is there who will not be moved when prayerfully meditating on, looking at, or imagining the Divine Savior hanging on the Cross! From the Crucified One we learn the overwhelming depths of God's love for us sinners, and the infinite character of Christ's spirit of self-sacrifice. Who will not love such a Lover! And by bearing our cross after Jesus, we shall obtain our crown.

Follower:

The sad thing today is that too few make the "Stations of the Cross" or meditate on Christ's sufferings as they recite the Rosary and recall the "Sorrowful Mysteries."

There are even those who fail to realize that the Sacrifice of the Mass is the living Memorial of the Sacrifice of the Cross! That is why we need the emphasis provided by your holy life.

Saint Paul:

I was born in Ovada, Italy and lived until a few years before the French Revolution. After a truly Christian education, I was favored with a devotion to our Crucified Lord.

I came to realize ever more clearly that I should found a Congregation whose members would particularly honor our Lord in His Passion. And so there came to be Passionist Fathers and Sisters of the Sacred Passion.

Follower:

You must have been very happy when Pope Benedict XIV approved the foundation of your Congregation and Rule. But you were more than a Founder. You were a mystic and a self-sacrificing missionary in Italy, while looking upon yourself as a sinner and a useless servant.

Saint Paul:

At the foot of the Cross, how can anyone remain cold and indifferent with respect to our beloved Savior! How can anyone remain proud when contemplating the freely chosen humiliation of One Who was both God and Man! And how can anyone fail to be sorry for offending such a Savior by personal sin!

Prayer of Saint Paul of the Cross

L ORD,
I give You thanks
for dying on the Cross
for my sins!

Follower:

Dear Saint, many today have lost the "sense of sin" and fail to appreciate what Christ has suffered to take away sin. They see no need for the Cross.

Teach us to bear our crosses out of loving gratitude to the Crucified Christ. Bring about

SAINT ALPHONSUS: MAN OF PRAYER AND ACTION—A man who made a vow never to waste, a moment, Saint Alphonsus accomplished a vast amount of work in his lifetime. But he ever kept before him the reason for all his action—union with his God.

a great change in Christians, so that they can truly be called Followers of the Crucified Lord.

✢　　✢　　✢

SAINT ALPHONSUS LIGUORI

Mystical Writer, Moralist, and Doctor

1696-1787　　　　　　　　　　　　　Feast: Aug. 1

Follower:

DEAR Saint, what an extraordinary Religious life you led—few persons have labored as much, either in word or in writing.

Devout from early youth, you became in turn a Priest after the will and example of Christ, a praying theologian, a spiritual director through word and writing, and a most devoted Bishop, for many years bearing a heavy cross and following the suffering Christ.

Saint Alphonsus:

I was blessed with a pious mother and father who helped me immensely. After becoming a lawyer, I was appalled by the lack of justice in the courts. One day I lost a case and it turned out to be my gain. I decided to become a Priest and quit the bar.

Many years later, I felt the urge to found a Religious Congregation. After much prayer to the Holy Spirit I founded the Congregation of the Holy Redeemer, known as the Redemptorists. Its purpose was to labor for the salvation of the most abandoned souls.

Follower:

It is well known that you met with great difficulties, but you were a most patient man in the sense of one who accepts suffering for a religious cause, for God's glory. You always labored prayerfully, and so work and prayer became spiritually one.

Saint Alphonsus:

I did my best to help as many people as possible. When I could not reach them by preaching to them, I had recourse to writing. I saw the need for a Moral Theology—so I wrote one.

Many persons do not know how to pray properly—hence I wrote about prayer, and so on. Ultimately, I had written about almost everything that was Christian.

Follower:

For more than one hundred years your works were read by countless Christians. They provided good reading that nourished souls and led to true Christian perfection.

The following prayer gives a good example of how you helped Catholics in their prayer life.

Prayer of Saint Alphonsus Liguori

O SACRED *Heart of Jesus,*
living and life-giving fountain of eternal life,
infinite treasure of the Divinity,
and glowing furnace of love,
You are my refuge and my sanctuary.
O adorable and glorious Savior,
consume my heart with that burning fire
that ever inflames Your Heart.
Pour down on my soul those graces
which flow from Your love.
Let my heart be so united with Yours
that our wills may be one,
and mine may in all things be conformed to Yours.
May Your Will be the rule
both of my desires and of my actions.

Follower:

Dear Saint, pray that Christians may once more read books like yours instead of being misled, de-Christianized, and demoralized by things they learn from books and other means of communication.

Help us to treasure good reading as one of the most effective means of learning to follow Christ and His Divine Spirit.

✣   ✣   ✣

SAINT GERARD MAJELLA

Lay Brother, Mystic, and Wonder-Worker

1726-1755   Feast: Oct. 16

Follower:

DEAR Saint, your wonderful life is an example of the value of manual labor when undertaken and carried out solely for God. In you it went hand in hand with mystical powers and astounding miracles.

Born in Muro Lucano in Italy, you lost your father when you were still very young. You suffered much in trying to be an apprentice tailor, but never complained. Your severe penances made you weak and unable to be accepted by Religious Orders. Finally, the Redemptorists accepted you, though grudgingly, as shown by the recruiter's remark: "I am sending you a man who will be a useless Brother." How mistaken he was!

Saint Gerard:

People, old and young, make mistakes—so it is all-important to practice patience with them. Youths are inexperienced and sometimes become enthusiastic for foolish causes. Some claim independence as a human right and others yield to evil passions.

Follower:

When we look at your life as a youth, we see with admiration that you advanced constantly in Christian virtues. And as a lay Brother, you put your hand to any kind of labor—sacristan, porter, gardener, infirmarian, and tailor. At the same time, you grew in spiritual wisdom to such an extent that you became the spiritual director for Nuns.

Saint Gerard:

I must admit that God did great things in and through me. Helped by Him, I did my best to be obedient and charitable, while taking great care to pray well and to practice mortification.

After my profession, strange things happened. I was able to discern spirits, performed miracles, and was fortunate that once a woman falsely accused me of immorality. This kept me humble.

Follower:

We know that you became an inspiration for your Religious brethren as well as for all who met you. When sickness afflicted you and tuberculosis exhausted you, you did not complain, nor grow lax in your spiritual exercises.

You became a follower of the Crucified Master, and joyfully bore your cross after Him. You developed a spirit of self-sacrifice for God's glory and for the salvation of souls.

Saint Gerard:

Be patient with youths and encourage them. Make pregnant women realize that abortion is murdering a child of God and that giving birth to a new child is cooperating with God, the Author of human life. As the patron of women with child, I will continually pray for them.

Prayer of Saint Gerard Majella

INFINITE *Purity,*
   I trust in You.

Keep me from every impure thought,
even the slightest,
which in my wretchedness
I might conceive.

Follower:

Dear Saint, when you died at the age of twenty-nine on the day you had foretold, you had already lived a full life for God. Watch over our youth and guard them from throwing their lives away at a young age.

Pray that the scourge of abortion will pass and all people will share your respect for life—both born and unborn.

✢   ✢   ✢

SAINT BENEDICT JOSEPH LABRE

Mendicant Pilgrim and "Fool of Christ"

1748-1783   Feast: Apr. 16

Follower:

DEAR Saint, you possessed a rather unique vocation—to be a wandering holy man of God, a "fool" of Christ. And as such, you bear eloquent witness that if need be we must sacrifice everything for God.

Born of a middle-class French Catholic family, you realized early in life that God was calling you to follow Christ in His poverty. There was no trace of pride in you nor of contempt for any person.

Saint Benedict Joseph:

I always tried to remember: "By the grace of God I am what I am." I came to realize ever better that the sole true evil is sin, for it offends an infinitely good God to Whom we owe all that we are and have. So I did penance for my sins and those of others.

At first I applied myself to studies, and did well in Latin. But when I reached the age of sixteen, I developed a distaste for the "natural sciences"; I then meditatively read the Bible, the inspired Word of God.

Follower:

You desired to become a Religious in a strict Order. You visited the Trappists, but they refused to accept you. You then turned to the Carthusians, but after a few weeks you realized that yours was a different vocation.

Saint Benedict Joseph:

I saw clearly that mine was an unusual vocation. I realized also that not only worldlings but good Christians would consider it improper to become what is variously called a tramp, a hobo, a bum. But I knew that the Lord wanted me to live in extreme poverty in a world in which many are money-mad.

Follower:

Many no doubt did ridicule you, perhaps even slammed doors on you, and kicked you out.

Saint Benedict Joseph:

I must confess that as I constantly recalled what our Lord suffered from His own people, I came to enjoy insults. I had the pleasure of visiting Rome and praying in various sanctuaries that brought to my mind the lives and deaths of Martyrs.

I was thus encouraged to bear witness to my Crucified Master by what I sometimes had to suffer. I must say many were kind to me, and I was accepted into a certain family where I was permitted to live a penitential life.

Prayer of Saint Benedict Joseph Labre

M*Y Lord Jesus,
may I mortify myself
and live for You alone.
May I accept all that happens*

as coming from Your hand.
May I always follow You,
and may I desire more and more to follow
    You.

Follower:

Dear Saint, you died at the age of thirty-five, just before the French Revolution, some of whose leaders tried to destroy the Church. This belied their cry of freedom, equality, and fraternity.

Though we are unable to follow you in your vocation, help us to follow you in preaching freedom from sin and the devil, equality among the children of God as created in His image, and fraternity based on His overwhelming love for us.

✢   ✢   ✢

THE BLESSED MARTYRS
OF COMPIEGNE

Faithful Religious and Followers of Christ

?-1794   Feast: July 17

Follower:

DEAR Mother Theresa, leader of this group of outstanding witnesses to Christ by your blood, your courage in the face of persecution and death is an inspiration to all Catholics.

You were victims of the cruelty and irrationality of human beings during the French Revolution, a time of unbelievable turbulence. For example, a prostitute was enthroned in the Notre Dame Cathedral of Paris, and some of the revolutionaries acted completely contrary to the chants of freedom, equality, and fraternity that rolled glibly off their lips.

Blessed Theresa:

In October, 1790, the National Assembly declared that all monastic vows were no longer recognized as existing. The law rejected them. After that, of course, monastic goods could be confiscated.

Follower:

The Carmel of Compiegne, of which you were prioress and which comprised eighteen Nuns, was "liberated." You were "permitted" to go into the new world of the "Enlightenment."

Blessed Theresa:

In 1792 we were told to live as private citizens. All the Nuns refused to renounce what they had solemnly promised to the Lord of heaven. We broke up into four groups and continued to live the Religious Life. We refused to proclaim allegiance to the new Constitution that went against our religion. As a result, we were cast into prison—in June 1794.

Follower:

By now your number had been reduced to sixteen. It is well known that you suffered many brutalities and indignities. You were haled before a revolutionary tribunal in Paris and every one of you, in turn, showed an exemplary Christian courage.

Blessed Theresa:

Humanly speaking, of course, we were fearful. But we also knew that we were condemned for clinging to our Catholic Faith. This meant that we were bearing witness to Christ and could rely on the help of His Spirit Who poured out the love of the Father on us. We entrusted ourselves completely to this living Triune God.

Follower:

What a marvelous witness you gave when you were brought to the place of execution—

singing in unison the "Hail, Holy Queen" and the "Come, Creator Spirit." The crowd of on-lookers became religiously silent at your courage. You were spiritually victorious in seeming defeat.

Blessed Theresa:

On reaching the scaffold, we each renewed our Baptismal as well as Religious Vows. Then each Nun went forth to what would bring us to the vision of our Divine Bridegroom, while all sang: "All you nations, bless the Lord. . . ." The chorus grew softer and softer until the last gave her life—and then there was silence!

Prayer of the Martyrs of Compiegne

PRAISE *the Lord, all you nations;*
glorify Him, all you peoples!
For steadfast is His kindness toward us,
and the fidelity of the Lord endures forever.

Follower:

Dear Blessed Theresa and Sisters who were her companions, you know the weakness of human beings and the offenses they commit against their God and greatest Benefactor.

Help us to overcome our weakness and turn always to God. Teach us how to be true followers of Christ, willing to sacrifice even our earthly lives for God's glory and the salvation of souls.

✛　　✛　　✛

SAINT JULIA BILLIART

Faithful Religious and Founder

1751-1816   Feast: Apr. 8

Follower:

DEAR Saint, after your holy death the Bishop of Namur said in admiration of you: "Mother Julia was one of those persons who can do more for the Church of God in a few short years than others can accomplish in a century." This is an apt summary of the kind of life you led and the goal of all your actions.

From your earliest years you were endowed by God with a wonderful intelligence and a profound inclination to holiness. You took a vow of chastity at fourteen but had to defer becoming a Religious in order to help your parents who were very poor.

Saint Julia:

The Lord was very good to me. This did not mean that He would not permit me to undergo sufferings. In fact, he wanted me to follow Him bearing a heavy cross, but one that He — as He always does when we accept our cross unreservedly—made light.

I was twenty-two years old when I witnessed the attempted murder of my beloved father, and became paralyzed in the process.

Follower:

Instead of becoming discouraged and inactive, you became even more fervent and engaged in a spiritual battle with the Jacobins, who during the French Revolution initiated the Reign of Terror. Your friends, the sixteen Nuns of Compiegne, were martyred at the guillotine.

When calm was restored, you founded the Congregation of the Sisters of Notre Dame, who are well known in Europe and in the United States.

Saint Julia:

I was helped by God's grace and by Father Joseph Varin. He founded the "Society of the

Fathers of the Faith," which took the place of the Jesuit Order that had been suppressed.

Follower:

The Notre Dame Sisters are known for their role as educators and for their work of giving religious instruction to children of very poor parents.

One striking event in your life occurred at the end of a retreat preached by a Father Enfantin, of the "Fathers of the Faith." You were suddenly and completely cured of the paralysis that you had borne without complaint for twenty-two years.

Saint Julia:

After that, God gave me the means to consolidate and expand my Congregation and its works. I worked hard to preserve what I considered to be willed by God, namely, the typically modern character of the Institute.

Prayer of Saint Julia Billiart

DEAR Lord,
    there seems to be no room for me on
    earth.
Please find a little corner in heaven for me
where I can be at peace!

Follower:

Dear Saint, you know the difficulties that beset many Orders and Congregations in our day. Vocations are scarce, morale is low, goals are in a state of flux, and operating costs are high.

Pray for our Religious. Teach them to rely on supernatural rather than natural means. Help them to effect a true renewal, founded on assiduous prayer, unwavering faith, and total fidelity to God and the Order.

✢   ✢   ✢

SAINT JOHN VIANNEY

Exemplary Shepherd of Souls

1786-1859   Feast: Aug. 4

Follower:

DEAR Saint, your life is a shining example of the fact that more things are wrought by prayer than this world dreams of. By dint of assiduous prayer and rigorous mortifications, you were instrumental in effecting the conversion of an entire village and untold thousands who flocked to you.

Born three years after the French Revolution, you were forced to practice your faith

SAINT JOHN VIANNEY: EXEMPLAR OF PASTORAL ZEAL—By an overwhelming love and unremitting pastoral zeal, Saint John overcame a lack of intellectual brilliance and became a priest after the heart of our Lord. He is the perfect exemplar of a dedicated parish priest.

secretly for a time. You decided to become a Priest but found studies difficult. Ultimately, you were ordained (at twenty-nine) more because of your devotion than because of your learning. Yet your practical knowledge of life and the Faith was incalculable.

Saint John:

I must admit that my heart sank when I was appointed pastor of Ars, a small village permeated with religious indifference and neglect. But I never lost trust in God.

His grace led me to spend many hours in prayer for my people, to do penance, to start teaching the children, and to preach powerfully against the vices besetting the town.

Follower:

Thousands came to hear your divinely inspired sermons and to seek forgiveness and guidance in your confessional, which became a "spiritual hospital." The devil expressed his hatred for you in fiery ways, but you repelled him with prayer and mortification.

Yours was a miraculous life, manifesting the power of God's grace when it finds no obstacle in a soul. You were a model of humility coupled with absolute confidence in God.

Saint John:

What you praise in me is in reality a praise of God. On your coins you have the expression "In God we trust!" If the majority of your people did that and became truly animated by the Spirit of God, your people would become outstanding in the world.

This renown would be yours not because you possess powerful nuclear powers of destruction but because you would be "armed" with the all-powerful love of God that is poured into souls by the Holy Spirit Who is given to us.

Follower:

You also had a lifelong devotion to the Mother of God. This reminds us that we are truly the children of the greatest of all mothers, the one glorified above all women.

Some of your fellow Clergy were envious of you and called you a fanatic, an ignoramus, a charlatan and even a madman. You forgave them, but your Bishop said, "I wish that all my clergy had a little of that madness in them."

Prayer of Saint John Vianney

B EHOLD *me,*
O my God.
I come to adore You,
to praise, thank, and love You,
and to keep You company
with all the Angels.

Follower:

Dear Saint, you know that our age sets a high price on knowledge of all kinds. But it sets little store on fidelity to commitments resulting from that knowledge.

Teach us the knowledge that you had— the Wisdom of the Saints. Grant that this simple and practical Wisdom will make us faithful to our vocation in life and bring us to loving union with the "Simple Man of Nazareth."

✠   ✠   ✠

SAINT VINCENT PALLOTTI

Religious Founder and Social Organizer

1795-1850   Feast: Jan. 22

Follower:

D EAR Saint, you were a forerunner of the Catholic Action Movement and set in motion a social program that was later elaborated and spelled out in a magnificent Encyclical by Pope Leo XIII—who happened to be a boyhood friend of yours.

Born in Rome, you earned doctorates in philosophy and theology and taught theology for ten years after your ordination. Then you branched out into the pastoral care of the poor, the sick, and the disadvantaged—becoming a second Philip Neri.

Saint Vincent:

I saw the need for assuaging the material needs of people before asking them to listen to spiritual things. So I spent my day making the rounds of all those places where the disadvantaged can be found—streets, hospitals, prisons—preaching and hearing confessions into the late hours of the evening.

I managed to obtain immense amounts of money and spent them for the good of the poor and the lonely. But I always tried to get them to help themselves, and I founded Guilds for this purpose.

Follower:

You knew that when we pray assiduously and with full confidence we can accomplish much for God's glory and the salvation of souls.

You were interested not only in forming Catholics in their Faith but also in converting Mohammedans. The latter unfortunately do not accept Jesus as the eternal Son of God nor do they accept to honor the Holy Spirit, the Spouse of Mary.

Saint Vincent:

When we are in heaven, we are no longer tempted to commit the sin of pride. There in God's presence we realize fully that by the grace of God we are what we are.

When you honor Saints, you honor God Who enabled them to do good. This fundamental truth was beautifully expressed by Mary when she received Elizabeth's praise: "[God] has done great things for me, and holy is His Name" (Lk 1:49).

Follower:

How great an inspiration you are for the Pallottines whom you founded and for the Sisters of the Catholic Apostolate. And we must add: the Mill Hill Fathers.

Prayer of Saint Vincent Pallotti

ETERNAL Father,
through Your infinite mercy
and through the infinite merits
of Your Divine Son, Jesus,
grant that You may be known, loved,
and glorified by all souls,
since it is Your holy Will
that all should be saved.

Follower:

Dear Saint, you know that even in our day of mass social welfare there are many people suffering and weighed down under inhuman conditions. Others are afflicted in the spirit.

Teach us how to assist their material wants so that we can then bring them to Christ Who will satisfy their spiritual needs. Let us know how to combine spiritual and material aid to the disadvantaged.

✢   ✢   ✢

SAINT PETER CHANEL

Exemplary Religious and Missionary Martyr

1803-1841   Feast: Apr. 28

Follower:

D EAR Saint, your life is an excellent
reminder that we belong to a Church that
is essentially missionary. This does not mean
that all Christians must go to the foreign missions, nor that we must be home missionaries.
It does mean that all should pray for missions
and missionaries and offer financial support if
possible.

Born in France, you were educated by a local
Priest and entered the Diocesan Seminary.
There both students and professors came to have
great esteem for you. You were an excellent student and a most devout Seminarian.

Saint Peter:

Because of the French Revolution there was
much disorder in the country, and some
parishes were in a sad state from the religious
standpoint. After my ordination I was sent to a
country parish that was completely run down.

With God's help, I instituted programs that
revitalized it in three years. But I felt called to

the foreign missions. So I joined the recently formed Society of Mary, known as the "Marists."

Follower:

But it was not God's plan for you yet. You were sent instead to teach at the Seminary of Belley. You spent five years there and did excellent work. You were a praying professor and had a very beneficial influence on the students.

Saint Peter:

I must admit that I was disappointed, humanly speaking, when I was not sent on mission. I learned, however, to be resigned, for it is always better to obey a Religious Superior than to insist on "doing one's own thing," as is said today.

For eventually I did get my wish and was appointed Superior of a small band of missionaries sent to evangelize the New Hebrides in the Pacific. After a ten-month voyage, we arrived and split up. I went to the island of Futuna with one lay-brother and Thomas Boog, an English layman.

Follower:

You were well received by the pagan people and even by their king. But when your winning ways gained many followers, the king became jealous and hostile. He did not care that you were bettering the people's condition. He cared only about removing your rival influence.

Saint Peter:

He sent some of his warriors and they quickly put an end to my earthly life by clubs. It all happened very fast, but I remember uniting myself with Jesus and joining my sorrows to His.

Follower:

It has been said that the blood of Martyrs is the seed of conversions. In your case, this proved perfectly true. Within five months after you had attained your wish to go to heaven, the entire island had become Christian.

Prayer of Saint Peter Chanel

L ORD God,
have mercy on me,
for I wish to go to heaven.

Follower:

Dear Saint, you know that we are immersed in the world and so are often tempted by the idols and false gods that have existed in every century. Keep our hearts free of them so that we can be imbued with God and proclaim Him to others.

Let us realize that evangelization, like charity, must begin at home, in the home of our hearts. Let us ready our hearts to be renewed continually and to act as missionaries in our environment. Remind us also to pray for the missions and for missionaries.

✢   ✢   ✢

SAINT CATHERINE LABOURE

Humble Instrument
of Mary Immaculate

1806-1876   Feast: Oct. 25

Follower:

DEAR Saint, your holy life was completely uneventful from a secular point of view. Yet because of a vision of Mary that was granted you, the lives of many Catholics were changed for the better. Unlettered in worldly knowledge and unappealing in worldly ways, you were still chosen by God and Mary to unveil a new devotion to the world.

Born in France, you did not attend school and learned to read and write only when you had reached adulthood. After your mother's death, you cared for your father until you became a Sister of Charity at the age of twenty-four. In the convent you received the series of visions of the Mother of God.

Saint Catherine:

Without warning I saw a lady seated at the right hand of the sanctuary. It was Mary. She told me, pointing to the altar on which our Lord was present in the tabernacle, that I would find much consolation there.

Follower:

Saint Bernadette was used by Mary to attract people to the "waters of Lourdes" and to her shrine at Lourdes. You had a rather different task.

Saint Catherine:

Mary showed me a medal representing the Immaculate Conception. As you know, that medal is now called the "Miraculous Medal" — because it was given miraculously and because it has been the instrument for miracles.

Our Lady told me to spread devotion through that medal. She instructed me to find guidance from a spiritual director. I realized how greatly I needed direction, for I was only a novice and a person with little experience in holy things.

Follower:

I have noticed that it so frequently happens that those who have received a particular commission must consult and obey a spiritual director. God loves to use weak instruments for teaching matters of Faith and for executing a particular work.

Saint Catherine:

I therefore transmitted Mary's message to my spiritual director and told him what I had seen and heard during three apparitions of our Lady. He arranged to have the medal struck according to Mary's instructions, and devotion to our Lady of the Miraculous Medal took root.

The devotion was fostered by Venerable Libermann, a convert from Judaism, who dedicated his missionary Congregation to the

Holy Heart of Mary. It had for its purpose to bring the Good News to the "most abandoned souls."

Follower:

But you, dear Saint, insisted on remaining unknown. Only after death was your name connected with this wondrous devotion.

You spent the rest of your life in obscurity, working as a portress in the poultry yard and serving the aged in the hospice run by your Congregation. What an example of genuine humility!

Prayer of Saint Catherine Laboure

O LORD, *here I am.*
Give me whatever You wish!

Follower:

Dear Saint, you have a marvelous lesson to teach our age. With God we can do all things, but without Him we can do nothing.

Inspire us to have true devotion to Mary, because she is an untiring advocate for us with her Son and with the Father. Make us repeat often: "O Mary, conceived without sin, pray for us who have recourse to you."

✝   ✝   ✝

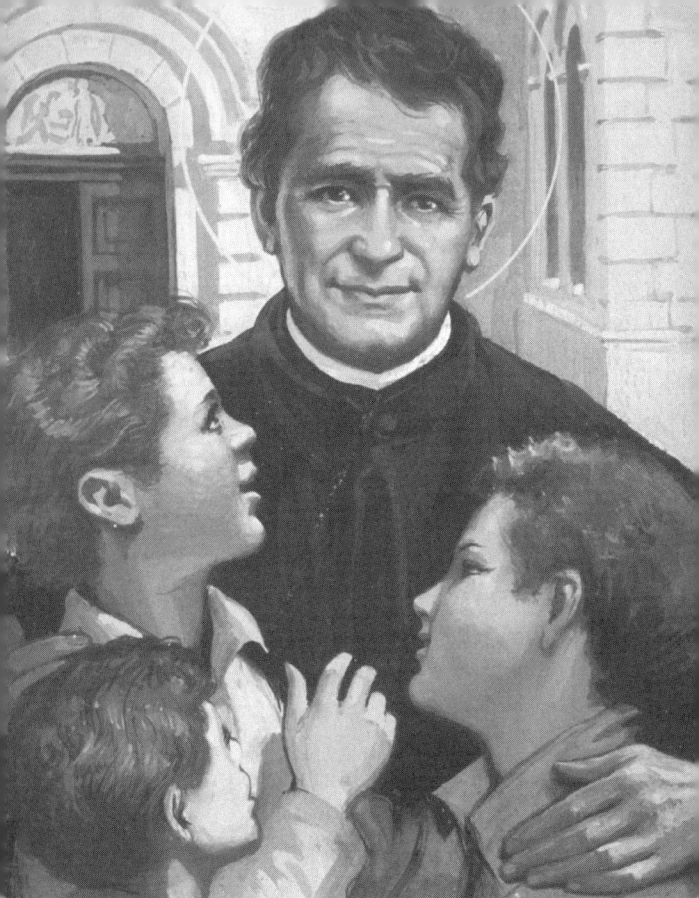

SAINT JOHN BOSCO: APOSTLE OF YOUTH—
Called by God to be the father and teacher of the
young, Saint John inaugurated an apostolate to
young people that is still going on. He combined
new educational techniques with love for God to
lead youth to Christ.

SAINT JOHN BOSCO

Apostle of Youth and Patron of Editors

1815-1888   Feast: Jan. 31

Follower:

DEAR Saint, the tone of your whole life of sanctity was dictated by your sincere and Christian love for youth. And it was by a life-long ministry to youth that you attained holiness.

Born only two months after the defeat of Napoleon at the Battle of Waterloo, you lived in Piedmont, Italy. Your country was still reeling from the after-effects of the Napoleonic wars and just starting to feel the pernicious (as well as beneficial) side-effects of the Industrial Revolution.

Saint John:

I was fortunate to have a devout mother who early taught me love for God and helped me get educated even though we were very poor. I was thus able to receive and embrace God's call to the Priesthood.

Once ordained, I soon became aware of the sad plight of countless city youths who were burdened with destitution, devoid of home influence, and deprived of religious instruction. You would call them "juvenile delinquents." But to me they were children of God, and I set up houses called Oratories where they had the opportunity to practice Religion—yet were never forced to do so.

Follower:

It has been said that your guiding principle was love and respect for each boy as a person. You thus evolved a system of preventive rather than repressive discipline.

You sought to make things attractive and you were an enlightened innovator in education. You also set up printing presses, wrote pamphlets about the Faith, and had the boys print them. In this way, they helped spread the Good News and at the same time learned a trade.

Saint John:

I always had great devotion to that mildest of men, Saint Francis de Sales. So I called those who came to help me *Salesians*. In time, they formed a Congregation.

Then I was aided by Saint Mary Mazzarello in taking care of homeless girls. Out of this came the *Daughters of Mary, Help of Christians.*

Follower:

You had unshakable trust in God. This gave rise to your calm approach to any problem. You always stressed the one thing necessary, as is shown by your motto: "Give me souls and keep the rest."

Saint John:

God was also good in giving me a love for the Blessed Virgin. She was the source of help in many situations.

Prayer of Saint John Bosco

M*ARY, powerful Virgin,
you are the mighty and glorious protector
of the Church.
In the midst of our anguish,
our struggles, and our distress,
defend us from the power of the enemy,
and at the hour of our death
receive our soul in heaven.*

Follower:

Dear Saint, you know how many of our youth today are still suffering from the effects of religious ignorance, destitution, and loss of family ties as well as from the unrelenting bad example given in the media.

Help them to turn to Christ and His Mother and change their lives. Teach us all to show them the kind of love you showed to such youth in your day.

✜　　✜　　✜

SAINT PIUS X

Pope of the
Blessed Sacrament

1835-1914　　　　　　Feast: Aug. 21

Follower:

DEAR Saint, you are known—and with good reason—as the Pope of the Blessed Sacrament. It is very clear that the giant strides taken in devotion to and frequent reception of the Eucharist in our day are the natural result of your initial impetus.

You allowed children to receive the true Bread that came down from heaven, Jesus truly present in the Blessed Sacrament. You urged frequent reception of Holy Communion—in a devout, respectful, and grateful way that leads to true Christian conduct.

Saint Pius X:

From my very earliest years I had devotion to Jesus in the Blessed Sacrament. Throughout my studies and my priesthood I carried it with me together with my other great devotion—to poverty. I was born poor, I lived poor, and I died poor.

When elected to the Papacy I was greatly afraid. But I put my trust in God and gave myself into Christ's hands—dedicating all my efforts *to restore all things in Christ.*

Follower:

Your accomplishments were many and world-shaking. In addition to changing the Eucharistic habits of Catholics for the better, you also renewed the Liturgy, gave great impetus to Bible studies, and effected the codification of Church Law.

Yet you showed yourself to be a true shepherd of souls: loving, self-sacrificing, eager to help those who were spiritually and materially in need.

Saint Pius X:

I was happy as a simple parish priest. God willed to make me Bishop and then Cardinal, but I never sought high honors. When I attended the conclave after the death of Pope Leo XIII I had a return ticket to Venice in my pocket—although I never had to use it.

Follower:

Your pontificate was one of the most pivotal for the Church—setting new norms for liturgical music, introducing a revised Catechism, and establishing the Confraternity of Christian Doctrine.

Saint Pius X:

The Lord called me to Himself at the beginning of the First World War. When will human beings decide to follow the Prince of Peace! When will they accept to live as creatures of the Heavenly Father Who invites them to become forever His children living in His heavenly home, where there is everlasting peace!

Prayer of Saint Pius X

O LORD *Jesus Christ,*
let Your Passion be my strength
to sustain, guard, and protect me.
Let Your Wounds be my food and drink
to nourish, fill, and invigorate me.
Let the shedding of Your Blood
cleanse me of all my sins.

Let Your Death obtain eternal life for me
and Your Cross lead me to everlasting glory.
Let these constitute for me
refreshment and joy,
health and uprightness of heart.

Follower:

Dear Saint, guardian of the Catholic Faith, full of sacred wisdom and apostolic zeal, inspire our spiritual leaders with similar zeal of working and suffering for God's glory and the salvation of souls.

Intercede for us that we may witness a new Pentecost when many will be following the guidance of the Holy Spirit sent by the Father and the Son.

✛   ✛   ✛

SAINT DOMINIC SAVIO

Patron of Youth

1842-1857   Feast: Mar. 9

Follower:

DEAR Saint, you were certainly outstanding in many things, and you can be of particular inspiration to young people. Although your

life was short when measured by years, it was long when measured by your spiritual accomplishments.

Young people can thus take heart from your deeds and be led to cooperate in good works. No matter how young a person may be, it is never too early to achieve union with God.

Saint Dominic:

I was born in Riva, Italy, in the very heart of the nineteenth century (1842) and was a fortunate recipient of God's generosity. Through His grace I was inclined to holiness, to doing good. One immense grace was my becoming a pupil of the great Saint John Bosco.

Follower:

It is most remarkable how in a very short time you attained such a high degree of perfection. You were humble, kind, and respectful toward legitimate authority. You were prayerful and ever ready to help others.

Saint John noticed these qualities in you and came to love you as if you were his son. You became his most zealous coworker.

Saint Dominic:

Prompted by the Holy Spirit and by Saint John, I realized that his Oratory needed better organization and good helpers. So I organized the "Company of the Immaculate Conception" to assist the work of the Oratory. This was shortly after Pope Pius IX had proclaimed solemnly as an Article of Faith that Mary was conceived without sin, conceived "immaculate."

Follower:

Let us not forget that you died at the age of fifteen!

Saint Dominic:

Of course, I did not become a Religious. I took no Religious vows but sought to practice —in accord with what our Divine Lord Himself so perfectly practiced—poverty, chastity, and obedience. I accepted suffering. And this in no way made me gloomy.

Follower:

Sadness does not befit Saints—or Christians for that matter! You knew that the sufferings of this life are not to be compared with the joys and the blessedness that God will give to His faithful in heaven.

But there are many sad young people today, because they want to find perfect happiness

where it cannot be found. Some even give
themselves up to suicide.

Saint Dominic:

Christ also expressed what is a great source
of joy and happiness even in this life: there is
more joy in giving than in receiving. Christ
was the most joyful one upon earth, for no one
gave as much as the Savior of the world.

Prayer of Saint Dominic Savio

O GOD,
  pardon my sins,
for I love You,
and wish to love You forever.
May this Sacrament,
which in Your infinite mercy
You permit me to receive,
blot out all the sins I have committed
by my hearing, sight, tongue, hands, and feet.
May my body and soul be sanctified
through the merits of Your Passion.

Follower:

Dear Saint, pray for our young people who
are daily deluged with many false philosophies
of life and countless temptations.

Make them realize that lovingly following Christ gives the greatest joy on earth and leads to everlasting happiness in heaven.

✢ ✢ ✢

SAINT BERNADETTE

Visionary of Lourdes

1844-1879   Feast: Feb. 18

Follower:

DEAR Saint, you had the privilege of seeing the Blessed Virgin Mary eighteen times when you were only fourteen years old. When you asked Mary to reveal her name, you heard her say: "I am the Immaculate Conception."

Your pastor found this a strange proclamation. Why did Mary not say: "I was immaculately conceived"? But you insisted on repeating what Mary had actually said. And in time, you found many who believed in your visions and your words. The world-famous shrine of Lourdes was the result.

Saint Bernadette:

I was an uneducated person. It came to my mind afterward that Pius XI had proclaimed on December 8, 1854, that we must believe as an Article of Faith that the Mother of Jesus Christ was conceived immaculate, without original sin. So Mary seemed to want to strengthen the faith of Christians in that truth through an ignorant girl.

Follower:

Christians who insist on basing themselves on the Bible alone and on the Bible as interpreted by each individual find it difficult to accept both the Immaculate Conception of Mary and her glorious Assumption into heaven, body and soul. The latter, we recall, was proclaimed by Pope Pius XII.

Catholics on the contrary accept the guidance of the Church Magisterium with respect to the interpretation of the Bible and they also accept the truths found in Tradition.

Saint Bernadette:

Our Lady also informed me about the "healing power" of the waters of Lourdes. This is what, as you know, is most in the minds of the sick who journey to Lourdes.

Countless miraculous cures have taken place there, but many sick who sought a cure did not obtain that favor. They often learned to accept their cross, which made them better followers of the Crucified Savior.

Follower:

Our Lord also let you suffer from illness. In 1866 you joined the Sisters of Charity of Nevers and there you manifested great patience and forbearance. Why did you not go to Lourdes to obtain a cure?

Saint Bernadette:

I realized that the "waters of Lourdes" were not for me. The Blessed Virgin used me as a broom to get rid of dust. When the work is finished we put the broom back out of sight, and there it is left.

Prayer of Saint Bernadette

O MY God,
   I beg You,
by Your holiness,
not that You may spare me affliction,
but that You may not abandon me in it.
When I encounter affliction,
teach me to see You in it
as my sole comforter.
Let affliction strengthen my faith,
fortify my hope,

SAINT FRANCES CABRINI: HELPER OF IMMI-GRANTS—Called to minister to the Italian immigrants of the United States, Saint Frances overcame problems of language, customs, finance, and prejudice to fulfill this ministry. Her secret was total reliance on Christ.

and purify my love.
Grant me the grace
to see Your hand in my affliction,
and to desire no other comforter but You.

Follower:

Dear Saint, teach us Christian patience. Make Catholics realize once more the great value of the devout meditative recitation of the Rosary.

In the Rosary we learn to be grateful and joyful for what is revealed in the Joyful Mysteries. In the Sorrowful Mysteries we recall how unbelievably good and self-sacrificing Jesus has been for us. And the Glorious Mysteries make us think of the blessedness of those who go to heaven.

✢   ✢   ✢

SAINT FRANCES CABRINI

Patron of Immigrants and Religious Foundress
1850-1917   Feast: Nov. 13

Follower:

DEAR Saint, you are an outstanding example of how God can do all things through His willing servants. As you were fond of saying, quoting Saint Paul: "I can do all things in Him Who strengthens me" (Phil 4:13).

The youngest of an exemplary Italian Catholic family, you helped your parents until their death. You then began teaching and working with orphans. You dreamed of doing missionary work in China and you founded the *Missionary Sisters of the Sacred Heart*—but you went to the United States instead.

Saint Frances:

God works in wondrous ways. He took a strict disciplinarian and autocratic woman like me, one with a narrow outlook and no religious experience, and dropped her into the cauldron that was the Italian immigrant's lot in America. In the process, His grace helped me to correct my faults, to become mellow, open-minded, and tolerant toward non-Catholics.

The more things I saw, the more I had to build schools, hospitals, and orphanages. The immigrants were surrounded by evils that have assailed others like them over the ages: lack of education, poverty, and ignorance of the language, conditions, and customs of their adopted country. And they were subjected to exploitation and antagonism on the part of the native populace.

Follower:

At first, you regarded your assignment as not hard enough and almost refused to go. But in time you saw that God was putting you in the place where you were most needed and for which you were most suited.

Saint Frances:

Once the work got under way, there was no stopping. I journeyed to Central America, Argentina, Brazil, France, Spain, and England as well as Italy and opened houses there. So many people needed our help and there was so much to do.

Follower:

You had great business acumen, and a practical knowledge of building as well as of hospital and school organization. In time, you also cared for others, such as the inmates of Sing Sing prison in New York.

Saint Frances:

But I always had before my eyes the One for Whom I was doing all this running around, the One for Whom I was involved in business and finance and a thousand details—Jesus, the Son of God made Man. I put all my hope in Him and asked His constant help.

Prayer of Saint Frances Cabrini

O JESUS,
    I love You very much.
I am being consumed by my love for You,
so that I am languishing and dying for You.
But despite such intense ardor,
I see and feel that my love is only a pale shad-
    ow
compared to the flame of Your love for me.
Give me a heart as vast as the universe
so that I may love You—
if not as much as You deserve—
at least as much as I can!

Follower:

Dear Saint, in our day, there are still ghettos—only they harbor other "immigrants." And all are afflicted by the same problems and the same temptations as those you assisted.

Help these new immigrants to turn to God. Teach us to look upon them as brothers and sisters in Christ and not reject them. Let us seek them out and help them.

✠   ✠   ✠

SAINT THERESA OF LISIEUX

Advocate of the Way
of Spiritual Childhood

1873-1897   Feast: Oct. 1

Follower:

DEAR Saint, your life is another glowing example of the fact that God often acts through humble persons and lowly things. You did not attain any honors, neither did you perform any world-shaking deeds. Yet you were a perfect vehicle for spreading God's teaching on the Way of Spiritual Childhood (or the "Little Way").

Outwardly, your life was uneventful and even boring. You served in your Order's laundry, sacristy, and refectory, and finally acted as a model novice mistress. Inwardly your life was one of surpassing spiritual beauty. You followed the way of trust and complete self-surrender.

Saint Theresa:

My parents, both of whom had desired to live a celibate life consecrated to the Divine Bridegroom, were exemplary Christians. After I lost my mother when I was five years old, I was reared lovingly by my father and my sisters. I also received great help from the Mother of Jesus who cured me of a grave illness.

Follower:

You became the precious pearl of a Carmelite Convent. Outstanding was your discovery and then your apostolate of Spiritual Childlikeness. This is not childlikeness in size or age but in a spirit of lowliness coupled with the greatest confidence expressed in total "abandonment" to God Who is Love.

You were only twenty-four years old when the Divine Bridegroom took you to heaven. How necessary are your teaching and example in our age of self-reliance and when there is a diabolically inspired rejection of the Lord and Creator of all.

Saint Theresa:

God knows perfectly what a spoiled child I was, spoiled, that is, because of all the unmerited favors and graces I received, first in my family and then in the Convent. "The mercies of the Lord I will sing forever" (Ps 89:22).

How well I was taught to embrace the heaviest crosses and accept the darkness through which I walked constantly toward the

end of my life when I continually repeated:
"Lord, I believe!"

Follower:

You climbed the heights of sanctity by the
dedicated performance of the little duties of
everyday life and the heroic endurance of petty
annoyances and ordinary hardships.

Prayer of Saint Theresa of Lisieux

O MY God,
   in order that I may be a living act
of perfect love,
I offer myself as a whole burnt offering
to Your tender love.
Consume me continually, letting my soul over-
     flow
with the floods of infinite tenderness
that are found in You,
so that I may become a martyr
of Your Love.

Follower:

Dear Saint, countless are those you prayed
for during and after your life upon earth.
Teach us all childlike confidence in and abandonment to the infinitely merciful God.

This is the best way we have of reaching that blessed life in heaven when, as we hope, we shall have the privilege to live forever in what we can call the Family of the Holy Trinity.

✢   ✢   ✢

SAINT GEMMA GALGANI

Stigmatic and Willing Sufferer for Christ

1878-1903   Feast: Apr. 11

Follower:

DEAR Saint, your life from the outside seems to have been one long period of suffering. As such it contains important lessons on suffering.

The existence of evil and suffering has plagued human beings for centuries. It remains a mystery as to why an infinitely loving God allows even most faithful followers of Christ to bear such heavy crosses.

Saint Gemma:

Saint Augustine, after his conversion, proclaimed that "there is only one evil and that is *sin."* Suffering is an evil in the natural order but it can be an occasion for good—for sanctification, for growth in Christlikeness.

All Christian Saints have learned to appreciate this fact as they meditated on what the Divine Savior chose to suffer for sinful human beings. The Stations of the Cross and the Sorrowful Mysteries of the Rosary provide ample material for meditating on our Lord's sufferings.

Follower:

You were born in Lucca, Italy, practically in our day. When you were twenty, you suffered a tuberculosis of the spine that doctors declared to be incurable.

However, through many prayers to Saint Gabriel you were completely cured, on the First Friday of May 1899. This date and day are clearly meaningful for us!

Saint Gemma:

I was grateful, of course, and sought admittance to the Congregation of the Passionist Nuns, but I was not accepted. The Lord then gave me extraordinary religious experiences. As the maxim goes, man proposes, but God disposes!

Follower:

Marks of Christ's Crucifixion appeared repeatedly on your hands and feet for over eighteen months, and in 1902 you became ill once more. The way the Crucified Savior wanted you to suffer in spiritual union with Him became known all over the world. You died a holy death in 1903 and were canonized by Pius XII in 1940.

Saint Gemma:

I came to see clearly that our Lord used me to show to the world that suffering can be a great means for self-sanctification and for completing in yourself what is wanting in the Sufferings of Christ—which at first seems a strange saying, but is what Scripture says (Col 1:24).

Prayer of Saint Gemma Galgani

DEAR Jesus,
help me for I desire to be good
no matter what the cost.
Take away, destroy, and utterly root out
whatever You find in me
that is contrary to Your holy Will.
At the same time,
dear Jesus,
illumine me so that I may walk
in Your holy light.

Follower:

Dear Saint, you know that there is still much suffering in our day. Unfortunately much of it goes to waste, so to speak, because it is not put to use for the sufferers' sanctification.

Teach us to recognize the supernatural value of sufferings accepted for God's glory and the eternal good of souls. May more and more people come to realize that *the real evil is sin*, which is an offense against the all-holy and infinitely loving God.

✛   ✛   ✛

SAINT MARIA GORETTI

Model of Purity

1890-1902   Feast: July 6

Follower:

DEAR Saint, your brief life and martyrdom come as a needed reminder in our "permissive" age. You bear eloquent witness that to yield one's bodily integrity without the sanctifying limits of marriage truly destroys the entire rhythm of the world.

Born in a village near Anzio, Italy, to dirt-poor but religious parents, you were a beautiful child, filled with love for God and your family. You were happy, good, open-hearted, without whim but with a sense and seriousness beyond your years.

Saint Maria:

Our family was so poor that my father had to share a piece of land and a makeshift house with another family—the Serenellis. I took care of my younger brothers and sisters while my parents worked the land.

There was great love and joy in our home. The only real regret I had about my poverty was that it prevented me from receiving my Divine Lord in Communion until I was eleven. This was because I lacked the proper dress for the King of Kings!

Follower:

Your poverty also made it impossible for you to have any formal education. But you learned the Catholic Faith from your devout mother and you learned about life from living it to the full for you were a bright child.

One of the two Serenelli sons was twenty years old and he developed a passion for you.

Twice he made sexual advances but you rebuffed him both times. But he warned you not to tell anyone or he would kill you.

Saint Maria:

Alexander was in the grip of the Devil and arranged for us to be alone in the house with only the younger children present. Then he tried once more to satisfy his lust. What could my answer be but no? I did not want either of us to sin.

He went into a rage and began to slash out with a knife. I do not remember much except that I woke up in the hospital. There the Priest gave me the Last Rites and also Communion. I was so glad to receive our Lord—it was only my fifth Communion.

Follower:

You were queried about your attitude to Alexander and replied that you forgave him. You also said that you were going to pray for his repentance and that you wanted to see him in heaven. Then you were received into heaven by your Heavenly Bridegroom, for whose love you had been willing to lay down your life.

Saint Maria:

I was especially glad to learn that Alexander after eight unrepentant years in prison was led by God to change his ways through visions of me. The grace of God is more powerful than any earthly force—all we need do is to be open to it.

Follower:

Indeed, Alexander was released for good behavior after twenty-seven years and begged forgiveness from your mother before becoming a Capuchin lay brother. He gave evidence at the canonical inquiry and lived to see you canonized. God's grace works miracles!

Prayer of Saint Maria Goretti

I CAN *no longer live without Jesus. How soon shall I receive Him again?*

Follower:

Dear Saint, you know that we live in a sexually permissive society, so that young people are dangerously confused about their sexuality. Help them to have a right attitude about this aspect of life that God has given us.

Teach all of us to be pure in life out of love for God, and to depend on God's grace in time of trial.

✣   ✣   ✣

SAINT MAXIMILIAN KOLBE

Apostle of the Printed Word
and Martyr

1894-1941   Feast: Aug. 14

Follower:

DEAR Saint Maximilian, it is rather fitting
that you are the last person treated in this
book. For you gave us a vivid example of love
for Christ and your fellow human beings that
cannot be surpassed. You willingly gave up
your life for another. You were our contempo-
rary, and you show that sanctity is still possible
in our day.

Born in Poland, you became a Franciscan
and earned doctorates in philosophy and theology. Yet your greatest works were of the practical order. You helped form a community of
800 men, largest in the world, even though you
were never free from illness.

Saint Maximilian:

Do not praise me. It was God Who gave me
the assistance I needed. And this all came to

me through our glorious Mother Mary. I had great devotion to her and strove to spread it to others. For she is the Mediatrix between us and Christ as Christ is between us and God the Father.

She remained my source of strength and inspiration throughout my life. In her honor I founded the "Immaculate Movement" and a popular magazine entitled "The Knight of the Immaculate."

Follower:

You traveled to Japan where you also built a monastery and then on to India where you furthered the Immaculate Movement. You believed firmly in the *apostolate of the printed word* and took steps to spread the faith through that word.

Saint Maximilian:

All my life I enjoyed communicating ideas to others. And I particularly enjoyed communicating the Faith to others. God in His goodness gave me the energy and the talent to accomplish a great deal for Him.

Follower:

In 1936, you were recalled to Poland because of ill-health, and when the Nazi invasion began you were imprisoned. After being released for a time, you were rearrested on a pretext and ultimately sent to that terrible concentration camp known as Auschwitz.

There you acted as a confidant to and comforter for the poor people imprisoned and fearing for their lives. You drew strength for this most difficult work by your close union with Christ and His Mother.

Saint Maximilian:

On July 31, 1941, a prisoner escaped, and as is done by all repressive regimes ten men were picked to die in reprisal. One was a young husband and father, who grieved for his family.

Suddenly, I felt impelled by God's Spirit to offer myself in his place. I heard my voice saying: "I am a Catholic priest. Take me in his place."

The authorities agreed and the ten of us endured days of slow death through starvation, thirst, and neglect.

As the last to die after ten days, I helped the others get ready to meet their Creator, and then I too was freed by death to go to meet our Lord.

Follower:

Your deed of sacrificing yourself for another was told round the world and was viewed as the culminating act of a life lived for God. In 1981, Pope John Paul II added you to the roll of the Saints.

Prayer in the Spirit of Saint Maximilian

*L*ORD *Jesus, You said:*
There is no greater love than this:
to lay down one's life for one's friends.
After the example of Saint Maximilian,
help us to offer ourselves
at least as spiritual sacrifices for others
by our lives and our works in union with You.

Follower:

Dear Saint Maximilian, you see how much selfishness there still exists among us. Teach us by your example to show our love for God by practicing good deeds for others.

Help us to realize that every good act done to another is an act done to Christ. And Christ will reward even the smallest act of kindness and self-renunciation done for others. For when we depart from this life the only thing we take with us is the record of our good deeds.

✝   ✝   ✝